Practicing Resurrection: The Gospel of Mark and Radical Discipleship

Janet Wolf

Practicing Resurrection: The Gospel of Mark and Radical Discipleship by Janet Wolf

For all other requests, contact
Director of Transformative Education
United Methodist Women
475 Riverside Drive, Room 1501
New York, NY 10115
Phone: (212) 870-3745
Fax: (212) 870-3736

ISBN: 978-1-940182-76-6

Library of Congress Control Number: 2018955520

Cover and interior design: Rae Grant
Cover image: Heidi Younger
Page layout: Nancy Leonard

Printed in the United States of America.

United Methodist Women Purpose

The organized unit of United Methodist Women shall be a community of women whose purpose is to know God and to experience freedom as whole persons through Jesus Christ; to develop a creative, supportive fellowship; and to expand concepts of mission through participation in the global ministries of the church.

The Vision

Turning faith, hope and love into action on behalf of women, children and youth around the world.

Living the Vision

We provide opportunities and resources to grow spiritually, become more deeply rooted in Christ and put faith into action.

We are organized for growth, with flexible structures leading to effective witness and action.

We equip women and girls around the world to be leaders in communities, agencies, workplaces, governments and churches.

We work for justice through compassionate service and advocacy to change unfair policies and systems.

We provide educational experiences that lead to personal change in order to transform the world.

{ Table of Contents }

Preface

> *Truly I tell you, wherever the good news is proclaimed in the whole world, what she has done will be told in remembrance of her.*
> —Mark 14:9

TOWARD THE END of Mark's Gospel, an unnamed woman interrupts a gathering of men in the home of Simon the Leper. The woman—uninvited, unwanted—anoints Jesus' head with oil, defying cultural and social norms, braving the grumblings of the male disciples. Jesus recognizes the unnamed woman and welcomes her in their midst. He receives the woman's anointment and then resoundingly affirms her faith saying, "Truly I tell you, wherever this good news is proclaimed in the whole world, what she has done will be told in remembrance of her" (Mark 14:9, Matthew 26:13). This affirmation is all the more astounding as this is the only time that Jesus insists a particular event must be included in the telling of the gospel. Wherever this good news, this gospel, is proclaimed Jesus says—wherever it is shared or lived, anywhere in the world—this woman's tender witness and radical discipleship will be remembered.

And yet, I was in divinity school before I first heard this story. If it had ever been preached in churches I attended along the way, I missed it. In truth, I was in divinity school when I finally realized all four Gospels portrayed women as central to the story of Jesus' ministry, crucifixion, and resurrection. I had memorized the list of twelve disciples—all men—as if they were the *only* disciples. I don't remember ever hearing the story of the audacity of the woman reaching out to touch Jesus' garment (Mark 5:25–34) or the holy boldness of the Syrophoenician woman (Mark 7:24–30) as examples of discipleship, of putting flesh on faith. And I know I had never heard these words of Jesus insisting that this woman in Bethany who anointed him was central to the good news. I had been in church my entire life and somehow missed this powerful piece of the Gospel for thirty-eight years.

I want to begin this study with the unnamed woman because of how powerfully it shifted my world as a woman to see a woman disciple for the first time. I want to ask throughout this study what might it mean to reclaim the stories of women as examples of radical discipleship? We know how women continue to be silenced, dismissed, written out of the story, and rendered invisible. We also know the power of stories to heal, transform, liberate, and unshackle. I want to begin with this unnamed woman as someone who reminds me to keep looking for who is left out, who is excluded and marginalized, who is being silenced or unwelcomed. In Mark, as well as the other three Gospels, faith and radical discipleship are embodied by the most unlikely people—people many of us have left out of the story.

We don't know who wrote Mark. Theodore Jennings, United Methodist elder, theologian, and seminary professor, chooses to use a female pronoun when referring to the anonymous author of Mark, noting that while we cannot know who the author was, we do know many women accompanied Jesus from the beginning to the end of his journey. Jennings writes that women have too often "been rendered invisible and anonymous by our male-centered histories, our male ecclesial leadership, our male academic and scholarly institutions. Thus, the pronoun 'she' serves fittingly to designate one who has deliberately chosen this, the lot of women, anonymity, even in the community of Christ."[1] Following Jennings' lead, I will use the pronoun "she" for the author of Mark as a reminder of the ways in which we silence, dismiss, and invisibilize women in the Bible and the church—the ways in which leftover patriarchy lives in us so that we are still startled by the female pronoun for a Gospel writer.

And there is a lot of leftover patriarchy! I grew up in a denomination that did not allow girls to collect the offering, read the scripture, or offer prayer during worship. Women were not allowed to be pastors or preachers. And even though my parents consistently told me I could be and do whatever God called me to, I was so steeped in this male-centered way of thinking that I bristled the first time I went to an ecumenical event and heard a woman preaching. I even actually remember thinking, "Who does she think she is?"

It was United Methodist Women who first shook me out of this mindset and encouraged me to imagine women as pastors and preachers, evangelists and effective worship leaders. And it was through a tiny United Methodist congregation that I found life and purpose, voice and vocation. While I had been active in the church from the beginning, and at an early age felt a very concrete call into discipleship, it was not until my life fell apart that I began to discover in my heart and soul, mind and bones, what wholeness in Jesus Christ might mean.

I remember one night in particular. My husband had walked out several months before, and I was struggling to figure out how I might survive as a single mom. I knew of absolutely no one who had been divorced, and I felt ashamed. I was up late that night, having put my two boys to bed hours before. While I could feel myself coming quite undone, I knew it was too late to call anyone. Besides, I had worn folks out with my ongoing cries of distress. I wanted answers they did not have, assurances they could not give. Sitting on the kitchen floor, broken by loneliness and feelings of inadequacy, failure, not measuring up, I suddenly felt in that moment a profound sense of God's presence surrounding me. There were no magic oracles, no voices from heaven, no assurances that I had answers. But that night I felt a certainty that no matter what, I would never be alone. I knew that I—even I—could be, had been, and would be again held by God's love.

The journey from that kitchen floor to finding my voice and vocation was a long and hard one that had a number of stumbling blocks. And without community, those who reminded me that I am named by God's good grace, I would not have made it.

I think about the first time I was invited to testify before a legislative committee about the potential harm caused by proposed cuts to welfare. As I remember it, I stood up and said something like, "I don't think you should cut welfare because I don't think you should and it's a bad idea." And then I sat down, embarrassed. Incredibly, the community of organizers did not give up on me, but instead invited me into the shared work of community organizing. Reflecting together—what to celebrate, what we might do differently next time, what concrete pieces we each would commit to doing for our next action—listened me into leadership.

This collective and participatory process showed me what being saved on the journey and what putting flesh on faith in Jesus looked like. It was in partnership with organizers—the women living in poverty, who were assaulted daily by racism and economic exploitation, patriarchy and other forms of violence—that I began to understand how my encounters with a liberating Jesus were inextricably tied to my sense of wholeness and to the liberation and wholeness of others. In the company of women struggling for justice and equity, in defiance of the harsh struggles just to make it through the day, I found life and laughter, healing and hope. I experienced the power of resurrection and the call into radical discipleship.

I write now with the conviction that United Methodist Women can lead the way in creating new partnerships and nurturing the partnerships already in action—partnerships that open possibilities for love and justice, life and liberation—by embodying radical discipleship in Jesus' name. We are in the midst of crises: poverty and famine; desperate refugees and immigrants searching for safety; climate change threatening our planet; rising economic inequalities; mass incarceration and mass deportation; devastating inequities in housing, health care, education, and employment; and relentless war and violence. There has never been a more urgent time for the church to really be the church of Jesus Christ. There has never been a more urgent time for United Methodist Women to embody radical discipleship in the name of the one who comes that all might have life abundant.

Where we stand, what we see, who we listen to, whose stories we value, whose voices we dismiss shape the way we understand the world and the Bible. For those of us immersed in the dominant culture of the United States, especially those of us who are white and economically secure, it can be difficult to hear stories that challenge our interpretation of the world around us. That is the power of ideology—it is everywhere and it is very powerful. It says over and over that there is just one way of looking at the world, that the dominant culture's narrative is the one and only right, accurate, and real version of the world.

I recall a time when I was a single mom with two boys and three part-time jobs. I remember signing up for a displaced homemakers program. During the first class, they asked me to write down where I wanted to be in ten years and I told them I wasn't sure I could imagine dinner that night let alone something ten years away. "That's the problem, Janet. If you don't know where you want to be ten years down the road, how are you going to figure out how to get there?" I realized they were speaking a different language from mine and I did not know how to translate it. They were living in a different world, and they could not imagine mine. Several years later I read a book by Philip Gourevitch in which he writes that power is "the ability to force others to inhabit their story of your reality."[2] I realized that was what had happened to me—those with power silenced my story by pulling me into their version of my reality. I realized they were not intentionally dismissive; after all, they were trying to help me. But they could not break through the walls of their own economic security and assumptions in ways that allowed them to really see or hear me.

If we are not in ongoing partnership with marginalized communities, if we have the "luxury of distance,"[3] it is too easy to forget what we have heard and seen when we do connect with communities that are struggling to get by. We need community to hold us accountable; we need authentic partnership with those who are hardest hit by the systems of injustice. If the world of impoverishment and systemic injustice is not our immediate reality, we are once again seduced into the established, old-order thinking of the world around us. Bryant Myers warns that we must "guard against the power of our education and experience. There is always a temptation to assume our view of reality is correct in a way that adds to the poverty of the poor."[4]

As a poverty-rights organizer, I had a conversation with a mother with two small children. She had come to ask for food and was painfully thin. Her children were unusually quiet and withdrawn. When she confided that she was six months pregnant, I was shocked. "When did you last eat?" I asked. "Two days ago," came the reply. And after a quick moment of sympathy, I rushed to explain the importance of eating while pregnant, the consequences to her baby's brain development if she did not eat properly. Her voice was almost a whisper when she responded, "I feed the ones whose cries I hear." More than forty years later and I am still learning and relearning the incredible force of social location and how quickly I forget.

The idea for this book is rooted in the realization of how much I need persistent proximity and partnership, and it is rooted in stories—stories that participants shared during interactive and participatory Bible studies inside prisons, on the streets, in battered women's shelters, and with congregations and among United Methodist Women.

Over and over again scripture has been broken open for me as I listen to a text with communities struggling hard for survival, communities for whom liberation is urgent and not theoretical. I am convinced that Bible study is still meant to be communal—the New Testament was written by, for, and with communities wrestling with what it means to be the church in a time of empire. Chilean scholar, liberation theologian, and priest Pablo Richard writes about what is often referred to as the "popular reading of the Bible," a community dialogue that reads the Bible "from below." He argues that we must ". . . reinterpret [scriptures] from the liberating perspective of the poor. This hermeneutical option for the poor is not artificial, for it is God's option, and it is normally the option of the biblical writers . . . The text has a new spiritual meaning when we become part of the text and the text becomes part of our life."[5]

Raised in the church and a leader in my home congregation, I was stunned by the pastor's words when I told him I had unwillingly become a single mom—two boys, three part-time jobs, and a husband who had left. Aching for someone to understand how much I hurt, how terrified I was of what was ahead, I was ambushed when he told me, "You are always welcome to worship here, Janet, but you realize you are no longer an acceptable role model so you will need to resign from your leadership positions." I had hoped the church would be a place of comfort during a time of crisis, but the pastor put into words the thoughts that had haunted my heart ever since my husband left: "You'll never measure up; there's something wrong with you; you're not good enough; even God finds you unacceptable."

My two boys and I left that congregation and began showing up at a church we had discovered two years earlier. I had sometimes taken children from a juvenile facility into our home on weekends—a brief respite from the damaging institution and a chance to be in a family with younger children, run in the woods, and choose the foods they might want to eat. Since most of the children who came to visit did not have dress-up clothes for church, we avoided our formal suburban congregation and worshiped at an inner city, multiracial, intentionally diverse house church located in an impoverished community. It was a church where most folks showed up in jeans and T-shirts, where music was accompanied by guitar, and children were anything but silent.

After the divorce, I was angry with God, prickly with still raw and decidedly difficult pain, and that little church loved me back into life. They put flesh on grace and created a safe space for us. Our first Christmas Eve with this congregation was approaching and we anticipated a celebration like the one in our suburban church: colorful pageants, a children's choir, and special music.

When they announced that Christmas Eve services were to take place at the state maximum security prison, I was not enthused. The pastor urged us to attend, emphasizing the story of incarnation, the Word becoming flesh among us, this baby born to an unwed teenage mama among an oppressed, colonized, and impoverished people. "This story belongs in the streets," he argued, "the body of Christ in and for and with the world."

When we arrived at the prison that night, though, we were told that we couldn't go inside. Something had happened at the prison, and we would have to hold our service outside. And even though this was Nashville, Tennessee, it was snowing. We were a sad little handful of people, huddled outside the immense prison, snow and sleet swirling around us. This was not my idea of Christmas Eve. Christmas Eve for me had included brilliant poinsettias and candles lighting up the rafters in the sanctuary. Christmas Eve was trumpets and pageantry, majestic music and bright colors, the choir spilling down the aisle, little children dressed up like angels and shepherds. Once we even had a live donkey. But here we were, standing in the cold. And I was pretty sure no one inside even knew we were there. My children were going to get sore throats and earaches and then I'd have to miss work. This was so definitely not my idea of Christmas Eve.

As all this went through my head, our group huddled together, trying to get the Christ candle lit. The fierce wind extinguished the match every time. A member of the group who was trying to help shield the flame handed me the Bible and said, "Read this." And I did, from Isaiah 9:2: "The people who walked in darkness have seen a great light . . . on them light has shined."

Just about that time, the Christ candle was lit and I leaned in, trying to help my children light their small candles. And still in my heart I was grumbling, sure this moment could not possibly matter to anyone. But then one of my boys tugged on my coat. "Mama, look!" I turned to look where he was pointing and saw, in cell after cell, the glow of matches and lighters being held up to the windows, light spilling through the bars. As we began singing "Silent Night, Holy Night" I imagined I heard voices inside and out, singing with the joy and awe of those who have turned to see what God is doing in the world around us.[6]

This was a formative glimpse for me into life-giving, Christ-centered, liberation-bound proximity, and to the power of the gospel from the margins. And I would have never gotten there on my own. I am grateful for all the individuals and communities who have nudged, prodded, pulled, and pushed me into being caught up in awe and wonder at the in-breaking of God's kin-dom[7] here, now, among us.

Most of what I think I know came to me through the gifts of other people—through community, through shared experiences and written texts, through academic study and engagement with the world around me. While I have tried to identify concrete pieces of this book that come from others, I also need to express gratitude to the many resources, written and lived, that have shaped my life and witness and go unnamed. A recommended reading list is included and will give the reader an idea of some of the written wisdom that has helped me along the way. I have put essential readings in bold. I am especially indebted to two well-known Mark scholars, Theodore Jennings and Ched Myers, who are both longtime friends, mentors, colleagues, and companions on the journey. I highly recommend their writings and work.

And I am grateful to Sarah Passino, a poet and community organizer, my friend and colleague, who worked with me in the editing process, who persistently and patiently pushed me into clarifying, simplifying, and revising this manuscript.

I write with a deep sense of gratitude for God's grace and the communities that have challenged and changed me along the way, the communities that have loved me into life and taught me what it might mean to share that large love, the communities that have held me through hard times and held me accountable. Communities that have converted and transformed me.

My chapters begin with words from Oscar Romero, the archbishop of El Salvador who was shot down by government-sanctioned assassins during worship on March 24, 1980. Romero's words are clear invitations into radical discipleship, a path he followed passionately and persistently. Converted by impoverished communities in El Salvador and by priests who dragged him from the sanctuary into the streets, Romero moved from being a quiet, politically uninvolved priest to an archbishop boldly exposing and confronting violent systems and the complicity of those in positions of power and privilege in El Salvador and the United States, the Vatican and the larger church. Romero walks alongside us through his writings, pulling us close enough to hear the cries of the people in the streets and to stumble into the Jesus who walks among and identifies with the impoverished and imprisoned.

One story that captures this spirit for me and that I share here in gratitude for all the named and unnamed teachers on my path is a story of one unnamed man in Nicaragua. He was sweating in the hot sun, tromping through the field in high rubber boots, a scarf tied around his forehead, dirt and grime layered on his shirt and pants. I introduced myself, shook hands, and asked for help in finding the pastor only to discover that he was the one I was looking for. This was the pastor who had accompanied people in their confrontations with and challenges to the repressive government. I tried to swallow my surprise. He said he was pleased to meet me and then he looked at me and asked, "Are you a Christian of title or conscience?"

This is a question that still accompanies me; it does not let me go. And this distinction of conscience—of radical discipleship, of faith-rooted living—is one I am not only so grateful to know, but am so grateful to see embodied and lived out all around me. I write with so many thanks.

I write with gratitude for all those who have pulled me from the sanctuary into the streets, including the little house church that loved me back into life at a time when I was a most-prickly person. They accompanied me as I struggled to find my voice and purpose and through them, in that community, healing happened. I write with thanksgiving for the women who led the poverty rights movements in Tennessee, women who challenged the overwhelmingly powerful and large systems and structures while struggling with economic exploitation and ongoing threats, while cradling babies and singing in the streets, while pulling me into the struggle so that I might find voice and vocation, purpose and power. I have deep gratitude for the congregations I have partnered with—for all that they taught me about the power of God's presence, the wideness of God's mercy, and the enough-ness of God's good grace.

I write with gratitude for SALT—Schools for Alternative Learning and Transformation—an ongoing think tank in a maximum security prison that reminds me over and over again that some of the most powerful theology, critical thinking, nonviolent strategy, and becoming-church takes place behind prison walls.

I write with gratitude for the Community Building and Conflict Resolution Circle on death row, a group with whom I have laughed and cried, struggled and hoped, as we work together for more justice than we have yet seen.

I write with gratitude for the bold and brave, fierce and fiery, militant but nonviolent organizers who have stood up and spoken out and who are naming, engaging, and transforming systems and structures, powers and principalities with prophetic love and grace.

I am especially thankful to Margaret Quern Atkins, Bill Barnes, Eric Brown, Rahim Buford, Garlinda Burton, Damien Durr, Jim Lawson, Ndume Olatushani, and Charlene Sinclair.

I am overwhelmed with deep gratitude for my family—my brothers, Tom and Jim; my sister, Glenda; and most of all, my parents, Dale and Clarice Wolf. They have taught us what unconditional extravagant love looks like when it takes on flesh and moves in among us. Deep gratitude to my wild and wonderful partner, Bill Haley, and to our five sons, Andy, Trey, Brook, Josh, and Ben; for their partners, Courtney, Virginia, Beth, and Cara; and our six grandchildren, Hallie, William, Pace, River, Niko, and Rocío.

I give thanks for the work and witness of United Methodist Women—for their invitation to write this study and for their consistent encouragement, support, and wisdom.

Love is infinitely more powerful than all the forms of death and I give thanks for all that is and all that is yet to come. As author Arundhati Roy writes, "Another world is not only possible, she is on her way. On a quiet day, I can hear her breathing."[8] To all those who have helped me listen long enough to hear her breathing, I offer thanks. And to those who continue to "craze me into holy awareness," I give gratitude and love.

Crazed into holy awareness

Come, Lord Jesus,
confront me as a prophet:
disturb my indifference,
expose my practiced phoniness,
shatter my brittle certainties,
deflate my arrogant sophistries,
and craze me into a holy awareness
of my common humanity
and so of my bony, bloody need
to love mercy,
do justly
and walk humbly with you—
and with myself,
trusting that whatever things it may be too late for,
prayer is not one of them,
nor a chance, nor change,
nor passion,
nor laughter,
nor starting yet again
to risk a way to be together,
nor a wild, far-sighted claim
that this human stuff of yours
is stronger still than fail or time,
graced to share a kingdom
and spirited for joy.[9]

ENDNOTES

1. Theodore W. Jennings Jr., *The Insurrection of the Crucified: The "Gospel of Mark" as Theological Manifesto* (Chicago: Exploration Press, 2003), 2.

2. Philip Gourevitch, *We Wish to Inform You That Tomorrow We Will Be Killed with Our Families: Stories from Rwanda* (New York: Picador, 1998), 48.

3. Denise Mina, *Deception* (New York: Little, Brown and Company, 2003), 45.

4. Bryant Myers, *Walking with the Poor: Principles and Practices of Transformational Development* (Maryknoll, NY: Orbis Books, 1999), 152.

5. Pablo Richard, Preface in *God's Economy: Biblical Studies from Latin America*, Ross Kinsler and Gloria Kinsler, eds. (Maryknoll, NY: Orbis Books, 2005), xvii.

6. A version of this story was published earlier: Janet Wolf, "To See and To Be Seen," in *I Was in Prison: United Methodist Perspective on Prison Ministry*, James Shropshire, Mark Hicks, Richmond Stoglin, eds. (Nashville: Abingdon Press, 2008), 111–112.

7. Please note the use of "kin-dom" in place of the traditional "kingdom." This term was first coined by Ada Maria Isasi-Diaz. It emphasizes relationality, community, and equity as the basis of God's reign.

8. Quote attributed to author Arundhati Roy, Good Reads, accessed December 28, 2017, goodreads.com/quotes/76282-another-world-is-not-only-possible-she-is-on-her.

9. Ted Loder, *Wrestling the Light: Ache and Awe in the Human-Divine Struggle* (San Diego: LuraMedia, 1991), 57.

Introduction

Gospel Good News: Turning the World Upside Down and Right-Side Up

We cannot segregate God's Word from the historical reality in which it is proclaimed. It would not then be God's Word. It would be history, it would be a pious book, a Bible that is just a book in our library. It becomes God's Word because it vivifies, enlightens, contrasts, repudiates, praises what is going on today in this society.
—Oscar Romero, November 27, 1977[1]

Mark's Jesus envisioned social reconstruction from the bottom up. His practice of inclusiveness and equality questioned all forms of political and personal domination. This Jesus called for a revolution of means as well as ends, enjoining his followers to embrace nonviolence and to risk its consequences.
—Ched Myers[2]

It is likely that our theological problem in the church is that our gospel is a story believed, shaped and transmitted by the dispossessed; and we are now a church of possession for whom the rhetoric of the dispossessed is offensive.
—Walter Brueggemann[3]

Rachel was a writer, and King, her husband, a physicist. We became friends after bringing our boys to camp on their property. They introduced us to the tradition of black-eyed peas and turnip greens on New Year's Day, hot water cornbread, and dancing in the rain. They taught the boys to drive a tractor and turn apples into cider.

The only time I saw King cry was when he talked about being listed as a communist during witch hunts led by U.S. senator Joseph McCarthy during the early 1950s. King said he would go to work every day but just sit at his desk—no longer allowed to do the work for which he had studied, trained, and been hired. Anyone who came to visit Rachel and King was suspected of being a communist and they were interrogated and harassed.

So, King and Rachel decided to reinvent their lives and move to a farm in the rural South. They would grow apples and peaches and start over in a new place. Being academics, they wrote to the United States Department of Agriculture (USDA) for information about starting and sustaining an orchard in rural Tennessee. They studied and then they talked with other people who had orchards. Somewhere in the process, Rachel decided she would like to have goats and so she wrote again to the USDA to receive instructions on how to raise and milk goats. "So, there I am," she explained, "the USDA pamphlet on my left knee, instructions underlined, and the warm belly of a bleating goat leaning into my right knee. And you know," she declared, "there's a world of difference between reading about something and actually encountering it in the flesh."

I love her story because it feels so familiar. For me, for a long time, the Bible was something I read from a distance; something not quite connected with my day-to-day life or the warm-bellied world around me. I read it on Sundays and special occasions, but believed I needed the help of someone with official authority to really understand it; I could not figure it out on my own. The Bible was old and comforting; it was somehow tied to my own personal salvation, to my individual morality, to my own comfort. I did not see the Bible as a window or a mirror into the world that I lived in. And then something shifted. Now, when I read scripture, especially Mark, it asks this question again and again: When and how does the Bible take on flesh? When and how do we move from reading the words on the page to encountering the living gospel, the good news, in our world?

I'm not sure exactly when this shifted for me. I probably go back to Rachel's story about the goat because it is such a good, clear picture of waking up to life around us, but I do have several distinct memories of parts of how this shifted for me that still catch my breath.

One memory in particular of the Word taking on flesh happened in the early 1960s when the country was in a struggle against segregation and other forms of white supremacy. My family moved from a small rural town in the North down to Atlanta, Georgia. We joined a large downtown church and my father soon became a leader on the church council. During this time, the civil rights movement was gaining strength and visibility. Downtown churches all over the city received notices from integration teams saying that they would come and attend worship with us. Our church had heated debates about this and after much wrestling, the congregation erected a small sign on the lawn in front of the church that simply said: "All who want to worship are welcome here."

When the designated Sunday arrived for the integration team to worship with us, they walked into the sanctuary, sat near the front, participated in worship, and then they left. Nothing felt dramatically different. But when we walked outside, we saw that the men from the congregation across the street were surrounding the church to make sure no one from the integration team could come on their property. Members from the integration team were physically threatened and pushed back into the street. And suddenly, the Bible moved out of the pulpit and into the streets; scripture took on flesh, and the carefully drawn boundaries of individual morality and personal salvation exploded. Suddenly, the Word came to life. All at once, I was encountering the gospel in the flesh: confronting the structures and theologies of oppression in me, in the church, and in the world around me.

And once I began to read the Bible—not from a distance, but up close and living in the world—it wouldn't let go. Reading the gospel this way pushes us to ask: Good news for whom? Good news about what? In Jesus' time good news for the Roman Empire was about Caesars' power and victories, about military conquests and empire expansion. But the good news, the gospel, that Jesus offers is a dramatically different kind of good news as Mark illustrates.

Good news in Mark is not Caesar's good news for the empire, for the powerful and privileged, but rather it is kin-dom good news for the impoverished and oppressed, for those pushed by systems until their "backs are against the wall"[4] and options for life are few. Mark's Jesus turns good news upside down and right-side up, and referring to Mark's author as a woman reminds us of this radicality. She tells us that good news begins *now*, bringing liberation, healing, freedom, wholeness, justice, and joy for all who are oppressed. Those complicit with oppression, those who cling to their power and privilege, will not hear this gospel as good news but as challenge and confrontation, as a disturbing demand for troubling transformation.

Mark, the earliest of the Synoptic Gospels, was written almost forty years after the crucifixion at a time when the early church was struggling, troubled, and traumatized. Many of those who had walked with Jesus were now imprisoned or dead. The First Jewish-Roman War of 66–70 CE ended with a destroyed temple and a fractured and frightened community. And then, as now, Christians were asking, what does it mean to be a disciple of this Jesus, crucified and raised?

Poverty was a harsh reality for most of the population, as it still is in our global world. Roman occupation, the presence of military troops, and the ongoing violence that accompanies economic exploitation and empire limited the possibilities for life. While sufficient resources existed, the systems of domination controlled and limited those resources, preserving the power and privilege of a few at the expense of the many. In direct challenge to these religious and political, economic and social structures and systems, Jesus provoked an uprising among those who were impoverished and oppressed—a movement for liberation and wholeness. This Jesus movement threatened those in power as Jesus repeatedly engaged oppressive powers.

While the particular systems of domination in our current historical moment are different from those during the time the Gospel was written, then as now domination defined the world and decided the distribution of resources. Today, more than one out of every three human beings lives in poverty without adequate resources. According to the United Nations Human Development Report, more than one billion people in impoverished nations lack access to health care and clean drinking water, to education and adequate food. More than twenty-three million refugees search for sanctuary in increasingly hostile environments, more than sixty-five million have been forcibly displaced. More than twenty-nine thousand children die every day from hunger and malnutrition, from poverty and related diseases that are entirely preventable. In the United States, one out of every five children live in poverty and that statistic changes to one out of every three for black children.[5]

Today, these inequalities play out in a world shaped by forces like the global political economy, a world in which the church has yielded much of its prophetic power. When Mark was written, religion was a major institutional force shaping the often-violent economic, political, and social reality of Roman-occupied Palestine. In Jesus' time religious leaders included the chief priests, some of whom were appointed by Herod, the Pharisees, Sadducees, elders, and the scribes.[6] Many of the religious leaders accommodated Roman politics and policies hoping to assure the safety and security of the Jewish people. They were convinced that compromise was the only way to survive. Some were complicit with the politics of oppression, hoping to win favored positions and accumulate wealth. There were religious leaders who were more interested in power and privilege, in control and riches, than in faithfully following God.

In reading and entering the gospel to better see and hear our world, it is important to remember that Jesus was Jewish; he identified as a Jew and he spoke, taught, ate, and walked with Jews in the Jewish community. Jesus was steeped in the sacred scriptures, in the practices of the prophets, the praying of the Psalms, the honoring of the commandments, the remembering of exodus and exile, the Passover and the Sabbath. The Jesus movement was rooted in these Jewish stories of the liberating God, the God who called together a people from among enslaved and oppressed "nobodies," the God who thundered in the harsh confrontations of the prophets with the powerful. The earliest church was made up of people who were Jewish and continued to be a part of the synagogue. There are always religious leaders who distort traditions and scriptures in order to prop up their own power, but too often Christians, by forgetting the historical contexts, distort the Gospels into anti-Jewish diatribes. Today, when reading the stories in Mark of Jesus challenging religious leaders, it is helpful to look around the world now at the Christian leaders who are collaborating with empire. We can understand the Bible better when we bring it into our world and into our streets; when we can see the back and forth between Jesus' challenges and our own, when we picture those who are leaders in the church now who value fortune and fame, power and prosperity more than faithfulness.

There is a story about my friend Will Campbell, a provocative theologian, Baptist preacher, and civil rights activist from Mississippi, being invited by a group of bishops to talk about inclusiveness. They had been confronted with the fact that almost all of the bishops were white men. People of color and white women challenged how this group could effectively represent a diverse body. As Will remembers the moment, he stood up in the huge sanctuary, looking down from the pulpit at the gathering of bishops who called him in to speak, and asked, "How many of you are willing to resign today so that women and men of color might replace you?" When no one raised their hand Will declared, "Well, if no one is willing to give up their position of power in order to move toward a more inclusive body, there is no point in having me talk about inclusivity." And he sat down.

For me, both the Gospel of Mark and Will's story powerfully frame the good news of Beloved Community and the hard and often uncomfortable, agitating work of seeing and changing personal and systemic holds on power. This *is* hard work. These positions of power are both inside of us and outside. We have internalized these hierarchies and they structure our imaginations and thinking, our institutions and nations. But, this is the sometimes unsettling nature of Mark—the author turns our world upside down, right-side up. To anchor this book as we move through the turns of this Gospel—the revolutions, the agitations—I offer the following keywords that I will use throughout for reading Mark:

Kin-dom: In keeping with the ongoing work of United Methodist Women and the subversive invitation of the Gospel, I use "kin-dom" rather than "kingdom" as a reminder that the Gospel unmasks and persistently resists patriarchy and empire and calls us into creating a new realm of relationship, a radically egalitarian, dramatically diverse, shockingly inclusive, justice-seeking, militant, but nonviolent Beloved Community that makes visible glimpses of God's kin-dom among us. Kin-dom is not rooted in king or tribe, but opens us to the multiple, overlapping, and ongoingness of relationships that reach toward justice. Referring to Mark's author as a woman reminds us of the Gospel's intentional delegitimation of all forms of patriarchal militaristic empire-building kingdoms.

Justice: From Genesis to Revelation, the Bible calls not only for kindness or good intentions, not only for reform of existing systems or charity, but for justice, God's justice, God's shalom. God's justice redefines social, economic, political, and religious systems and structures. It is distinctly different from charity—though charity at its best, requiring persistent proximity, leads to justice. God's justice requires a radical reorientation, moving us from programs and projects designed by the privileged into partnerships with those who are oppressed; from ministry *to* or *for* those who are dispossessed into ministry *with* those who are struggling. It moves us from domination into collaboration and from authoritarian hierarchy privileging the voices, stories, values, and decisions of the powerful, into doing theology from the bottom up. God's justice radically reorients and moves us toward privileging the voices, stories, values, and decisions of those who are oppressed by structural violence.

Liberation/Salvation: In Mark, people and communities are saved, liberated, set free. They are healed through faith that takes on flesh and the prophetically powerful presence of Jesus Christ. Salvation is not only individual, but also communal; it is not a one-time event but an ongoing process. To be saved is not simply to be assured of some residence in heaven after we die, but to be liberated here and now from all the powers of death and domination, for abundant life and radical discipleship. This salvific, liberating Jesus is not content to remain in some otherworldly realm of heaven; this Jesus shows up in the middle of the most brutal struggles, weeps with the women at the foot of so many crucifixions; this Jesus marches in the streets, rides the bus with impoverished maids, accompanies the oppressed in the fields and kitchens, hollers in the halls of power, and turns over the tables of the privileged.[7]

Radical Discipleship: Radical discipleship is an orientation, not a program. Radical discipleship takes freedom—our collective freedom—as both object and method. Following in the path of Jesus requires individual and communal discipleship that unmasks, names, engages, and transforms the forces of death, the systems and structures, the theologies and institutions of death-dealing powers and principalities. It calls us toward a militant nonviolent struggle among, and in partnership with, those who are oppressed. It moves us towards communally creating a visible alternative to the domination system, a reflection of God's kin-dom.

I have offered these working definitions of keywords above not as fixed meanings, but as touchstones. Their definitions are shifting, deepening, inevitably breaking open something new in me. As Howard Thurman, an African-American prophet and pastor, poet and nonviolent practitioner who fueled the theology and witness of Dr. Martin Luther King Jr., reminds us: we must always be mindful of where we sit in relation to power. These keywords help anchor me in this question. Thurman wrote:

> *Too often the price exacted by society for security and respectability is that the Christian movement in its formal expression must be on the side of the strong against the weak. This is a matter of tremendous significance, for it reveals to what extent a religion that was born of a people acquainted with persecution and suffering has become the cornerstone of a civilization and of nations whose very position in modern life has too often been secured by a ruthless use of power applied to weak and defenseless peoples.*[8]

These keywords offer a lens for exploring together what it might mean for United Methodist Women to expose the ways in which our congregational practices and policies prop up the powerful and oppress those who are most vulnerable. How is it that we can attend worship regularly, be active members in our churches, and somehow still end up supporting so many death-dealing systems? White supremacy in the United States is often theologically justified by the silence and complicity of the church, embedded in our theology, in our worship and Bible study, our committees and programs. The School of the Americas Watch defines white supremacy as "an historically based, institutionally perpetuated system of exploitation and oppression of continents, nations, and peoples of color by white peoples and nations of the European continent, for the purpose of maintaining and defending a system of wealth, power, and privilege."[9] Even before Constantine's official wedding together of the sword and the cross or of the military victory and the gospel, Christians struggled with our compromise and complicity with the systems and structures that defy God's kin-dom and the gospel. In the United States, it is common for churches to have American flags in their sanctuaries, something that would shock congregations in South Africa or Nicaragua.

Theodore Jennings emphasizes the urgency of Jesus' invitation to radical change in Mark and the challenge the author puts to us to expose and confront the ways we have compromised, become complicit. Jennings asks,

> Have we not, in fact, so compromised our commitment to the mission of Jesus that we have actually sought to defend ourselves, establish ourselves? And has this not led inexorably to our securing our personal and institutional existence through collaboration with the very forces that are opposed to God's solidarity with the poor and broken? . . . Have we not become the chaplains of a system utterly at variance to the reign of God?[10]

In Mark, discipleship is this fierce and "holy impatience,"[11] an unwillingness to continue with business as usual, with getting by, with going along with the way things are. Twenty-seven times Mark, the shortest Gospel, uses the word "immediately" (NRSV). Mark pushes us forward, pushes us out the door, and pushes us into the streets. We hear her push expressed by what Dr. Martin Luther King Jr. referred to as the "fierce urgency of now," a decisive moment in which we must respond. In his April 4, 1967, speech, "A Time to Break Silence," Dr. King says that we have to face the fact that "tomorrow is today." He goes on to tell us that we are "confronted with the fierce urgency of now . . . We must move past indecision to action. We must find new ways to speak for peace . . . and justice . . . Now let us begin. Now let us rededicate ourselves to the long and bitter—but beautiful—struggle for a new world."[12] Already radical transformation is possible, Mark and King point out; it is happening now among us.

Jesus, the Jewish teacher rooted in the prophetic Hebrew traditions and scriptures, moves among the impoverished and oppressed peoples of Palestine, stirring up a nonviolent movement in defiance of state and religious authorities. And Mark writes not to convert unbelievers, but to challenge and transform the church. Theologians Theodore Jennings, Obery Hendricks,[13] and Ched Myers[14] note, Mark is a "manifesto" for radical discipleship. Jennings, in *The Insurrection of the Crucified: The "Gospel of Mark" as Theological Manifesto*, explains how he sees in the wholeness of Mark the text's "potential to confront and convict," and how he considers "this gospel as manifesto—a public, political argument that provokes a response—for, here, one who is crucified still lives, still calls us to radical discipleship, to insurrection against all that diminishes life, to a vision of a new society in which all may thrive."[15]

In the shower on the second floor of our house, there is a small high window that looks out into the tops of trees and a slice of the sky. When I told my husband what a wonderful job he had done planning this window so we could see sky, passing clouds, and the tops of trees he laughed. I am 5'9" and he is 6'4". He was quick to point out that my view is not his view, which is full of wires, telephone poles, shingle roofs, and a radio tower. Both of us tell the truth of what we see out the window, but our truths come with dramatically different views.

This is true for all of us. We are shaped by what we see out our windows and our front doors from our particular perspective. This is one of Mark's invitations: the author shows us the power of social location; she offers us a contextual theology. This is a lesson that I keep having to learn: in the shower, in my communities, out in the streets. I come back again and again to Mark because the author teaches us to identify our own power and privilege, to name the place from which we are seeing the world. Where you stand determines what you see; whom you listen to determines what you hear.

I'm inside a maximum security prison, and it's time for our closing circle. I ask people to offer up their names and one thing they are grateful for today. "This circle." "Community." "One more day." "My children." "Challenge." And then it comes to Frederick, recently released from death row after the overturning of his conviction. "My name's Frederick and I give thanks for grass."

"Really?" I think. "We are in this serious space, about to leave after a powerful and thick two-hour discussion and you want to give thanks for grass, for pot, for dope? Really??" That's what I'm saying in my head but what comes out of my mouth is, "Do you want to say more about that?"

"Sure," Frederick responds. "When you're on death row, the only way you get outside is in the cage: concrete floor, wire on all sides.

And every single person in that cage tries to reach out and touch the grass. You can't do it. It's just out of reach. But I don't know anybody who doesn't try. Over and over again, I'd stretch out my hand and think if I can even touch one tiny piece of grass, man. But you can't. So now I do. Every day I get up, I give thanks for grass."

When Devon, a member of our Community Building and Conflict Resolution Circle, has his conviction overturned and he is moved from death row to the low side, he falls into the grass, stuffing the wet green into his mouth and his pockets, rolling over and over in the grasses' leaves and laughing. The guards let him. They know. Everyone inside knows: all those years, just waiting to touch the grass.

Left to my own assumptions I almost always get it wrong. I will assume everyone sees the same view I do out the shower window, I will assume I know what "grass" means when I hear someone in prison talk about it, I will just *assume*! But Jesus pushes us in to community; he pushes us to change our location so that we are present with those who suffer—and then to translate that presence into partnership in ways that challenge and unmask our assumptions, biases, stereotypes, and misconceptions. Jesus in the Gospel invites us to see, to really see, people with their "backs against the wall"[16] and to know that if we do not, our map of the world will always be incomplete; that we will miss the mark.

Think about where most of the biblical stories take place: Africa and the Middle East. What color are people who are indigenous to most of the countries in Africa and the Middle East? Brown, black, olive. What color are their eyes? Brown, black, dark. And yet, most of the images of Jesus in the United States still reflect the historically impossible blond-haired, blue-eyed, pale-skinned Jesus. Most cultures do create images of the divine in our own likeness. The problem is when we come to believe these are the only acceptable, accurate, true images or perspectives.

For a long time, biblical studies pretended to be objective—to provide the one right meaning of a text. This is one of the reasons that Mark is such a gift—why radical discipleship offers such a transformative framework—it gives us a way to move beyond this as a question about individual morality. The "objective" view of the world was fundamentally wrong because it was built on a foundation that did not see most of God's children. The good news Mark brings is this: if we all look together, if we lift up and privilege the voices of those hardest hit, those targeted by the systems, oppressed by the conditions of our day, then we can begin to see God's kin-dom! The earlier scholars were not bad—they just gave us a view of a very small world; they gave us a view out of their shower window that we now recognize as a predominantly white, overwhelmingly male, mostly upper-class academic view of what turns out to be a very un-objective world. This Western worldview distances, dismisses, and silences the voices of much of the world, especially those on the underside of history, those struggling to get by. As Virgilio Elizondo, a Mexican-American theologian and priest, labor activist and professor, writes, "There is something in the colonized identity of the Galilean that people who have never been colonized do not suspect. There is something which the poor and exploited . . . of the world have perceived that the powerful of this world have missed."[17]

But I am not sure if I could have heard Elizondo without first being in partnership with folks who had their backs up against the wall, just like I am not sure if I could hear Mark's author and her invitation without also being in community with those struggling just to get by. This is the invitation to radical discipleship that Mark offers. With these together we can ask how our social location—who we are, where and how we live, our race and ethnicity, age, gender, education, economic circumstances, language, sexual identity, family of origin, physical abilities, geographic locations—shapes our hearing of the gospel and our understanding of who God is and how God is at work in the world. The gift of radical discipleship offers a view of the vastness and largeness of God's world.

Moses and the people of Israel were delivered from enslavement into freedom, from Pharaoh's brutal oppression into a journey that would lead to the Promised Land. They experienced God as a deliverer, liberator, provider and as a freedom-fighting, covenant-creating God. But Pharaoh and his army had a different story to tell. Good news may not feel or sound like good news to everyone involved. Good news to those who have privilege may come first as a challenge, a call to risk; good news may come as a hard and unsettling call to repentance instead of an easy embrace or comforting promise.

It is my hope that this book will provoke critical thinking and communal participatory immersion into the biblical texts. But this is not an easy journey. The author of Mark is clear about the difficulties of discipleship, but she is also amazingly concrete in her images of encountering Jesus as liberator and responding to Jesus' call to radical discipleship that gives us the freedom to live out and work for God's kin-dom with our whole selves, here and now.

Invitation to a Spiritual Growth Journey

Readers are encouraged to set aside time each day to enter into Mark's Gospel with the expectation of encountering a liberating, and often startling Jesus. It is perhaps helpful to use a journal to record your journey, your questions along the way, your fears, anxieties, hopes, joys, and discoveries.

I am a sometimes meditator, which simply means a person who sets aside time, sometimes, to listen and to try to connect with the silence inside by moving through the noisy distractions and unending lists of things to do. Sometimes this occurs during a walk in the woods or by a lake, but most often it happens in a corner of my study. I sit in a chair with my feet on the floor and my hands resting lightly on my knees. If thoughts come—my list of things to do, my stewing over something that has happened—I acknowledge them but imagine waves carrying them out to sea and then settle in to the silence. Much of the time there is no surprise or no sudden revelation, simply a renewed sense of centeredness and an awareness of God's presence and movement in the world around me, a feeling of gratitude. Sometimes, though, images pop up during my mediations as if someone has ambushed me with a story. These are often startling, unexpected, and every now and then, they are disturbing.

I remember one such image. I was walking along a shore at the edge of the water, soft waves washing over my bare feet. I could hear someone in the distance calling but could not make out the voice or person. I was staring down at the sand, marveling at the reflection of early morning sunlight on the waves, when I was startled by a man briskly walking past me. He turned briefly, just as he passed, and said simply, "Come." I cannot tell you exactly why I decided this was Jesus, but I did, and so I turned to follow only to find myself caught, struggling with heavy chains that weighed me down.

As this Jesus figure moved farther and farther down the beach, I hollered, "Can't you see I can't come? All these chains are holding me down; I am unable to move, quite unable to move." And then the Jesus figure turned his face to me and from a distance said, "Let go."

And then I realized I was holding the chains tight in my hands. As soon as I let go, they slid off; I was free.

Dorothee Soelle, German liberation theologian, author, and activist who joins Mark in revealing the social contexts of our theologies, has helped me to identify the chains I hold on to so that I can learn to let go of these chains and find freedom. She extends an invitation to ask ourselves what it might mean to encounter Jesus as liberator and ourselves as whole persons freed by our encounters with Jesus. In her book *The Silent Cry: Mysticism and Resistance*, Soelle encourages readers to adopt three daily practices I include here that continue to shape not only my reading of Mark but my day-by-day living.[18]

Practice Amazement

First, we are to practice amazement: to be caught up in wonder, to be awakened to the gifts of God's good creation and the power of God's presence. We must practice amazement, Soelle argues, because we are all too often trapped in the smallness of "customs, viewpoints and convictions." We cannot think apart from these, we cannot imagine a world without these systems of domination—of patriarchy, empire, white supremacy—that shrink our worlds, that diminish our capacities to be fully alive and awake. We have been numbed, anesthetized, lured into sleepy unawareness.

Mark emphasizes amazement that breaks through our biases and blinders, that shifts our assumptions and theologies, and opens us to the kin-dom spilling out among us: ". . . they were all amazed and glorified God, saying, 'We have never seen anything like this!'" (Mark 2:12).

Every day we should practice amazement, breaking through the numbness to notice and celebrate beauty, to be caught up in awe, to awaken ourselves to the good gifts around us. Linda Zralek, a friend and poet writes, we can't perhaps know everything about God, but surely, she says, "we catch glimpses / hear rumors, see signs and wonders / and now and then, touch the hem / of her garment."[19]

It is helpful to me to jot down at least one very concrete moment of amazement every day. And it is best to be more specific than noting "the sunrise this morning," but instead, "the fiercely red sky splattering light through the window to splash sunrise on my feet; the grin on Rahim's face when, after twenty-six years in a cage, he steps through the gates of the maximum security prison and begins dancing in the sunlight." The Syrophoenician woman in Mark 7 who defies the men's efforts to silence her and, by her persistent faith, changes Jesus; the unnamed woman in Mark 14 who anoints Jesus with oil, embodying a faith that we can see. The moment when, after months of organizing, calling, letter writing, storytelling, testifying, we hold our breath as the final vote is taken and then erupt in raucous shouts and cheers, as it becomes clear that millions of people in the United States will, at least for now, have access to affordable health care.

Unlearn and Let Go

Soelle's second invitation is to unlearn and let go. Unlearn the ways of empire, the seduction of consumerism, the web of lies that props up power and privilege, and let go. Every day we will discover something we have been taught, some belief we have held on to, some particular way of looking at the world around us, some behavior that must be unlearned and released. For many of us who are white, it is an unmasking of the racism inside us, and an acknowledgment of the power and privilege whiteness brings to us. This unlearning and letting go must be a daily practice. Over and over again in Mark's Gospel, we are confronted with our need to unlearn and let go of the logic and practices of empire and the web of lies perpetuated by the domination systems.

For many of us, we will bring this unlearning and letting go again and again to our encounters with scripture. With our worlds cracked open, we will return to a scripture passage we have read a thousand times, and it will be new as we learn to keep asking who benefits from this interpretation and who may be harmed. For example, when we spiritualize poverty and argue that everyone experiences poverty in some way, we silence the necessary and sharp critique of economic exploitation, of the violence of systemically perpetuated poverty. Without unlearning and letting go—daily, as we live—we allow ourselves to define sin through the lens of our own biases, to follow the categories of kingdom over the prophetic truths of our shared kin-dom.

Resist in Order to Heal

Finally, Soelle teaches us that every day we must resist in order to heal and heal in order to resist. Once our unlearning and letting go exposes the powers of domination at work within us and in the world around us, Soelle argues that we can heal through resistance and "change death-oriented reality." We can actively resist the systems and structures, theologies and practices of death in the world around us and become co-creators with God in the ongoing creation. In our resistance to death-oriented living, we become partners in healing and hope, resurrection and new life. We become freed to be fully human, liberated for kin-dom living and loving here and now.

We resist in order to heal. We resist the cynicism of our times and the notion that we really can't change the way things are. We resist any sense of powerlessness, so that we might heal and uncover the power God has already given us. Soelle gives us this practice to transform our own lives and so the world; our resistance ripples, we all learn to let go of our chains.

These three practices are an ongoing journey. Every day when we practice amazement, unlearn and let go, and resist in order to heal, we welcome the kin-dom of God and we welcome the radical good news of the gospel erupting in us and in the world around us.

I remember an old black-and-white short film with sound but no discernible words. In my memory, the film opened with an obviously important wealthy man striding about his property instructing a smaller man, who appeared to be some kind of servant, on the care of the workers and the fields.

The large landowner then turned to the workers in the field and I could tell they were asking for something, taking off their straw hats, showing the landowner empty plates and gesturing for food. The man turned his back, walked higher up on a hill and stood over them, lecturing to them from what was clearly a Bible, repeatedly pointing his finger to the text and then shaking his pointed finger at the workers. The workers were hunched over and silent, growing smaller as the man continued his stern lecturing. The wealthy man then abruptly closed the Bible, turned away from the workers, and walked inside a glass house. He sat down inside the house and ordered the servant to bring him a meal. The servant began to set up an elaborate table—tablecloth, flowers, an abundance of plates and silverware, wine, water, and foods. Periodically the man would shout and gesture and the servant would bring more.

Meanwhile, one of the workers picks up the Bible the man has left on the bench, and begins to read. Soon he calls other workers over, excitedly pointing to text after text, page after page. The workers become animated, totally engaged, and suddenly begin to smile and dance. They move toward the glass house and are almost at the door when the landowner turns and sees them. They lift the Bible and point at passages so the man can see but there is no response. They again make gestures asking for food and lifting the Bible so the landowner can see but the man will not look. Instead he motions to the servant to lower the blinds.

This goes on for some time and, while we can see inside the house, the man can no longer see out. He has had the servant pull everything possible to block doors and windows and still he orders more food and wine. The trash piles up, there is no way for the servant or the man to get out of the house now, barricaded as it is, and so no way to get rid of the trash or leftover food.

Eventually between the workers knocking on the doors and windows and the man's trash and debris piling up inside, the house cracks and crumbles into tiny pieces. The last we see, the workers are digging the man out from under the rubble, brushing him off and offering him a glass of water.

This story stayed with me as a challenge and an invitation. An invitation to ask how I close out the cries of those around me, how I use the Bible to justify the way things are instead of listening to the biblical texts and those struggling to challenge and change me, so that we together might challenge and change the systems and theologies that perpetuate oppression. And it is a reminder for me that those pushed farthest to the edge are most often those for whom the Bible and this liberating Jesus are indeed good news.

Invitation to Communal Spiritual Growth through Participatory Bible Study

The Bible was written by, with, and for communities who collectively wrestled with God's engagement with the world and who we are called to be as the people of God. It is in this spirit that I offer the following communal Bible study process. Participatory Bible study is not nearly as predictable or orderly as a Bible study led by a teacher who has decided on the content before the gathering. However, this process is incredibly powerful to help us hear the radicality of the gospel and call us each and together into radical discipleship. I have used this process with groups of six hundred people and with groups of six. While I have often been surprised, startled, challenged, and changed, I have never been disappointed in its power to awaken people, including me.

Choan-Seng Song is a United Methodist pastor and seminary professor, story-theologian and author who writes "theology from the womb of Asia," challenging Western-centric orthodoxies of individualism rooted in capital and empire. Song notes that Jesus offers a new way of doing theology with and among the people of the land—the impoverished and oppressed. Song writes, "Jesus tells stories and speaks in parables, stories and parables taken from the life of the people with whom he shares daily problems and difficulties. Jesus does theology of God's reign with them and does not do it for them. He develops it out of them and does not impose it on them. He empowers them to experience it and to claim it."[20] My hope is that we too will do theology among and with those who are living with their backs against the wall.

Doing theology with folks whose backs are against the wall means that we have to show up, that we cannot rely on programs, on easy fixes, or on easy answers. It asks us to see each other and ourselves in relation: to the world, to systems of power and privilege, to the wall. Today, African-American scholar Vincent Harding's writing on this is helpful to begin. He writes:

> *. . . those people who live most obviously with their backs against the wall—for instance, the homeless, the working and jobless poor . . . the alienated, misguided, and essentially abandoned young people—are rarely within hearing or seeing range of the company of Jesus' proclaimed followers . . . And those wall-bruised people find no space for their presence in the places where the official followers are comfortably at worship . . . those whose wounded backs and spirits testify to the continuing reality of the walls.*[21]

In this book, I recommend that Bible study groups work to create partnerships with communities that are struggling. These partnerships should be mutual, long-term relationships in which we listen to and learn from and with each other. For many of us in the United States, that would mean relocating ourselves so that we leave the isolation of our sanctuaries and move into the streets and harsh realities of so many communities. Consider partnering with those who are inside a jail or prison, inside a shelter for battered women, or those who are homeless, or in an immigrant or youth detention center. It is most powerful if half of the Bible study participants are from the outside and half from the jail, prison, shelter, or detention center.

At least one of the facilitators should be an insider (resident of jail or prison, shelter or detention center) who will co-facilitate with an outsider if there is one. This process will not work if the facilitators are seen as assigned leaders in charge of framing not only the questions, but also the answers. The facilitators are meant to be "animators." Their goals are to break open space for the radicality of the gospel to be engaged. A facilitator "raises eyes and loosens tongues."[22] The facilitators will need time to listen to the text and become familiar with the process of participatory Bible study. Facilitators are encouraged to learn about the social, political, economic, and religious context of the biblical text so they can raise questions that invite participants to wrestle with the text, to dig deeper, and to see the texts as mirrors of our world.

If it's not possible to relocate outside church walls, consider partnering with groups led by those who have been caged or trapped by the criminal justice system, excluded by the economic system, or excluded by the church itself.

Members of the group need not have the same faith background, nor do they need to all be Christians in order to engage the story. In my experience, it is often people who are unfamiliar with Christian scriptures that raise the hardest questions and bring the deepest insights to the texts.

The framework:

1. **Circle Process:** Arrange the chairs so that people are sitting in a circle. Explain that circles are a part of ancient practices honoring collective wisdom and acknowledging the value of everyone's voice and participation. Circles allow us to create a community of equals. Circles remind us that everyone is a teacher and everyone is a learner.
2. **Opening Circle:** Begin the conversation by having one member of the group ask an opening question. It should be something simple, perhaps what gift you bring to this space today or what is one thing you are grateful for today. The question should be something everyone can answer. Ask each person to offer the name they want to be called, no titles, just names, and then their brief response to the question. Remind people that even though we may know someone's name, when a name is spoken it is an invitation for others in the circle to offer silent gratitude for the gifts and participation of that person. Saying our names aloud each time also very practically builds in a radical hospitality so that we can intentionally fold in new members of the community when they arrive and they will feel seen and welcomed.
3. **Community Guidelines:** Create community guidelines together by asking for a popcorn response (one or two words offered quickly, one person after the other, as the words come to mind) to the following: "What do you need and what will you offer others in order to make this space safe? What do we

need for this to be a space where each person can bring their authentic self?" Write the responses on a chalkboard or poster paper. Ask participants to be brief, but take time to clarify what people mean by the words they add. For example, if someone says "confidentiality," ask what is meant by that so that everyone understands that what is said in this space stays in this space unless we have the speaker's permission to repeat it elsewhere. After about five minutes of brainstorming together, ask if any of the words or phrases need clarification. Then ask if everyone in the circle is willing to be held accountable by these community guidelines. If there are problematic suggestions, work to clarify them so that the group reaches consensus and everyone agrees to honor and be held accountable by the community covenant. Make sure someone records the notes so you can come back to them each time you meet. It is helpful to have someone type the notes so that everyone has a copy of the covenant by the second meeting. Confirm that everyone agrees to everything on the list and that this then is the community covenant.

4. **Small Groups:** The facilitator identifies the characters or groups in the study text and, while prioritizing diversity and even distribution, asks participants to choose where they want to be in the story. For example, for the passage discussed in Chapter 1 of this text, Mark 2:1–12, you might have four or five groups: the man on the mat, the group that carries him, the scribes, Jesus, and, if you have enough people, the crowd. If you only have an hour for this process, small groups might meet for twenty minutes and perhaps spread around the room or location. If the group is large, you can have several groups for each identified character or group in the text so that there are no more than ten people in a small group, preferably seven.
5. **Invitations and Assignments:** Read the text aloud and share instructions before participants break into their small groups. Make sure they are clear about their assignments:

a. Each group will choose: a facilitator to help the group stay focused and make sure everyone is included in the conversation; a notetaker to keep track of the group discussion; and a reporter to help the group frame and focus their report back to the larger group.
b. Spend ten minutes immersing your group in the story from your character or your group's perspective. What is going on in your head and heart? Why do you do or say what you do? What scares you? What threatens you? What gives you hope? Joy? Do not hurry through this part of the process—do not explain anyone else's behavior or any overall themes from the text. Focus on who you are and what is happening with you.
c. Spend five minutes engaging in the larger story. Ask how this particular text holds a mirror to our world—what do you see through the lens of your character's social location?
d. Spend your last five minutes asking, "So what?" What does this story provoke in you? How has it broken you open, challenged or changed you, and why does that matter? Ask for concrete answers to the questions: what does it look like to respond to the challenges of this story? How does this story invite us into the radical discipleship of walking with Jesus into kin-dom, kin-dom living and loving here and now?

6. **Reports:** After twenty minutes of small group discussion, ask everyone to come back into the larger circle. Invite each group to bring their report to the whole group, in whatever way they want. This is the moment of greatest challenge—and the greatest gifts—for the large group facilitators, as they will need to pull threads from the reports to focus the discussion and conversation. Be ready for surprises, humor, and hard truths. Invite the groups to respond as reports are being made but focus first on asking who each group is and why they do what they do. Only after those initial reports, grounded in the world of each character or group, will the facilitators move the conversation to the present

and ask where we see our world in the text and, most importantly, to name the stakes, addressing the question "so what"?

7. **Closing Circle:** End your time together with a closing circle: Offer your name and a brief response to a question that everyone can answer. For example, what gift do you take from this time together? Remind people to offer silent gratitude for each person as they say their name.

Carlton Wilkinson created a photo series entitled "On the Altars of Liberty" exploring the role of churches in the civil rights movement. One of the photographs was taken in Dexter Avenue Baptist Church, the congregation where a young Dr. Martin Luther King Jr. served in his first pastorate. The photographer took the photo from behind the pulpit. An open Bible is just in front of the camera, and we see an empty church, rows of empty pews, and unstained glass windows providing a peek into the streets outside. When I look at this image, I think of all the people who stand behind pulpits, opening the Bible, contemplating what text to read, what words to offer, and I think of the power of the prophetic word, the lingering challenge of Dr. King's witness as he writes in his "Letter from a Birmingham Jail":

> *Wherever the early Christians entered a town the power structure got disturbed and immediately sought to convict them for being "disturbers of the peace" and "outside agitators." . . . The contemporary church is often a weak, ineffectual voice with an uncertain sound. It is so often the arch-supporter of the status quo. Far from being disturbed by the presence of the church, the power structure of the average community is consoled by the church's silent and often vocal sanction of things as they are . . . I am thankful to God that some noble souls from the ranks of organized religion have broken loose from the paralyzing chains of conformity and joined us as active partners in the struggle for freedom.*[23]

Carlton's photograph and Dr. King's words give me strength to engage Mark with an open and courageous heart.

Using This Text for Personal Growth

At the end of each chapter is an opportunity for you to reflect on the content and how you can apply it to your life. This section, titled "Personal Reflection: Wrestling with Radical Discipleship," contains additional information, reflection questions, and ways to apply what you have learned. The following are some suggestions for how you can get more out of this study as an individual:

1. Read the Gospel of Mark from start to finish in one sitting. Do this several times. My friend and distinguished Mark scholar, Theodore Jennings, suggests we do so and then ask: "What would we say about Jesus if this is all we had to go on, if these were the only stories handed down?"
2. Use a journal to jot down reflections, images, stories, and notes about your encounters with the stories in Mark, with this particularly disruptive and demanding Jesus.
3. Read the focus texts in each chapter of this study before reading that chapter so that you come to the stories with your own experience and ideas before you enter into the conversation that takes place in this book.
4. Define your social location by naming your citizenship status, geographic location, gender, age, education, race, ethnicity, family of origin, economic status, marital status, sexual identity, language, and physical abilities. Then, identify what gives you privilege, power, and status in your location.
5. Reflect on how your social location impacts your hearing of and response to the Jesus of Mark.
6. Begin a daily practice of practicing amazement, unlearning and letting go, resisting in order to heal and healing in order to resist.

7. Practice the participatory Bible study process. If you are someone with power and economic stability, this is possible to do without changing social location, but it is highly recommended that you engage the voices and stories of those with their backs against the wall, if not in person at least through readings, videos, and/or films.
8. Spend time making a plan of how this new knowledge will spur you to take action in your own community.

ENDNOTES

1. Oscar Romero, *The Violence of Love: The Pastoral Wisdom of Archbishop Oscar Romero*, compiled and translated by James Brockman (San Francisco: Harper & Row, Publishers, 1988), 13.

2. Ched Myers, Joseph Nangle, Cynthia Moe-Lobeda, et. al. *"Say to This Mountain": Mark's Story of Discipleship* (Maryknoll, NY: Orbis Books, 1996), xv.

3. Wendy Robins, ed., *Through the Eyes of a Woman: Bible Studies on the Experience of Women* (Geneva: World Council of Churches Publications, 1995), 29.

4. Howard Thurman, *Jesus and the Disinherited* (Boston: Beacon Press, 1996; first published by Abingdon Press, 1949), 11.

5. "The State of America's Children 2017," Children's Defense Fund, accessed June 4, 2018, childrensdefense.org/library/state-of-americas-children/2017-soac.pdf.

6. Thurman, 20.

7. A more thorough discussion of these ideas is found in Chapter 5. As Jacquelyn Grant, womanist theologian and professor, notes in her groundbreaking book *White Women's Christ, Black Women's Jesus: White Feminism and a Womanist Response.*

8. Thurman, 11–12.

ENDNOTES *continued*

9. Elizabeth Martínez, "What Is White Supremacy?" School of the Americas Watch, accessed, October 15, 2017 soaw.org/component/content/article/108-race/482-what-is-white supremacy?tmpl=component&print=1&page.

10. Theodore W. Jennings Jr., *The Insurrection of the Crucified: The "Gospel of Mark" as Theological Manifesto* (Chicago: Exploration Press, 2003), 153–154.

11. Ibid., 29.

12. Martin Luther King Jr., "A Time to Break Silence," in *A Testament of Hope: The Essential Writings of Martin Luther King, Jr.*, ed. James Melvin Washington (San Francisco: Harper & Row, Publishers, 1986), 243.

13. Obery Hendricks Jr., *The Politics of Jesus: Rediscovering the True Revolutionary Nature of Jesus' Teachings and How They Have Been Corrupted* (New York: Doubleday, 2006), 319, 330.

14. Ched Myers, *Binding the Strong Man: A Political Reading of Mark's Story of Jesus* (Maryknoll, NY: Orbis Books, 1988), 11f.

15. Jennings, xii.

16 Thurman, 11f.

17. Virgilio Elizondo, *A God of Incredible Surprises: Jesus of Galilee* (Lanham, MD: Rowan and Littlefield Publishers, 2003), 5. It is important to note that Elizondo was accused of molesting a boy during his time as a priest. Elizondo committed suicide more than thirty years after the accusation, though he had repeatedly denied the charge. I have included his quote but want to emphasize that doing so does not ignore the possible harm he inflicted. It seems to me that his work is still valuable and that it is possible to learn from this man who was often referred to as one of the key theologians in Mexican-American religious thought. As Bryan Stevenson, Equal Justice Initiative, comments, "We are all more than the worst thing we have ever done."

18. Dorothee Soelle, *The Silent Cry: Mysticism and Resistance* (Minneapolis: Fortress Press, 2001), 90–93.

19 Linda Zralek, *I Drink Beauty from Any Cup* (Nashville: idjc press, 2015), 33.

20. C.S. Song, *Jesus and the Reign of God* (Minneapolis: Fortress Press, 1993), 132.

21. Vincent Harding, Foreword in Thurman, *Jesus and the Disinherited.*

22. I heard this phrase used by Anne Hope and Sally Timmel, popular educators and authors of the four-volume series, *Training for Transformation: Handbook for Community Workers* (London: Practical Action Publishers, 1996). These volumes come out of faith-based community development organizing in Zimbabwe and provide powerful resources for participatory democracy and leadership.

23. Martin Luther King Jr. "Letter from a Birmingham Jail," in *A Testament of Hope*, 300.

Chapter 1

Radical Discipleship: Mark 2:1–12

When we struggle for human rights for freedom, for dignity, when we feel that it is a ministry of the church to concern itself for those who are hungry, for those who are deprived, we are not departing from God's promise. God comes to free us from sin, and the church knows that sin's consequences are all such injustices and abuses. The church knows it is saving the world when it undertakes to speak also of such things.
—Oscar Romero, December 18, 1977[1]

Unfortunately, brothers and sisters, we are the product of a spiritualistic, individualistic education. We were taught: try to save your soul and don't worry about the rest. We told the suffering: be patient, heaven will follow, hang on. No, that's not right, that's not salvation! That's not the salvation Christ brought. The salvation Christ brings is a salvation from every bondage that oppresses human beings.
—Oscar Romero, September 9, 1979[2]

During divinity school, I had the opportunity to spend six weeks with base Christian communities in Nicaragua. I had read about base Christian communities and was struck by their similarity to the early church. They are churches of the poor located in struggling communities that give flesh to a radical equality among members of the community where everyone is considered a "delegate of the Word" and no one person is identified as leader or pastor or priest. Base Christian communities, like the early church, practice the radical discipleship of challenging, confronting, and transforming the powers of death in their communities; they practice resurrection. Liberation theology—which privileges the voices and experiences, the wisdom and witness of those who are impoverished and oppressed—took on flesh in these communities. I watched as these communities in struggle and in the footsteps of Jesus became visible alternatives—counter-narratives—to empire.

Being the good Methodist that I was, I was methodical in preparing for my time in Nicaragua. I read books and articles, corresponded with members of base Christian communities—I contacted professors who wrote and taught about this particular form of church. Before I went, our family hosted members of base Christian communities from Central America in our home and church, and I interviewed delegates of the Word, immersing myself in the theology and witness of these communities.

Then the day came for my first worship experience with a base Christian community in the mountains of Nicaragua. As I walked up the hill toward the house where worship was to take place, I felt my heart sink. The house was filled to capacity. There was no room for anyone else to enter. And then I remembered that most houses in Nicaragua do not have glass windows or even screens but only shutters, and these shutters were open so I could hear and see what was happening inside. No problem.

As I moved closer to the house and an open window, I saw a chicken perched on the windowsill. Clucking and picking away at something on the sill, the chicken seemed unimpressed by my efforts to shoo it away. "That's okay," I consoled myself, "I can still hear and see."

Then children began to call to one another from opposite sides of the nearby road. I could feel my impatience increasing as I strained to listen to the community inside. And then the children chased a pig between me and the window and the clucking chicken. And I felt my temper explode as inside my mind I shouted, "I have come all this way, spent all this time preparing for this moment; I have my camera, my notebook, my tape recorder ready. And for what?" A man standing nearby turned to me and commented, "It is good, is it not, to celebrate God's presence in the midst of the people!"

And standing there with him I realized that it was not that I had forgotten what I learned earlier and was just now remembering it.

It was that I all of a sudden realized that I could read all I wanted and not fully learn what this meant—for people to gather, to become the church in the midst of all the holy noise of the world—until standing there, together, not in a silent sanctuary, but in the middle of a Holy Spirit happening right here in the streets. A Jesus kind of church: poor folks crowding around, hungry to hear and participate in the good news. Mark 1:15 tells us: "Now is the time!" (CEB). Not just some time in the past or in the future, but here and now the kingdom, the kin-dom of God is at hand, breaking in.

This passage in Mark 2, the story of a community tearing through a roof in order to create possibilities for healing, invites us into a radical discipleship, a base-Christian-community kind of church, a brush arbor, a black-prophetic-church-tradition kind of church, a John-Wesley-in-the-streets kind of church. Mark here reminds us we are called to a different kind of discipleship than most of our new member classes might describe. As biblical scholar Lee Camp writes, the call to radical discipleship reminds us that radical

> *. . . means "to the root." And it is in this sense that the Christian faith is radical: it demands thoroughgoing transformation, thoroughgoing conversion, of every realm of human endeavor, in personal relations, economics, and politics, in homes, culture, and social order. The gospel demands radical discipleship . . . not a call to a burdensome moral perfectionism, but a call to leave the old ways of death and darkness, to walk in the new way of abundant life and glorious light with the Christ who is Light and Life.*[3]

As always, it is not merely helpful but is a prophetic demand to listen to the gospel with communities in the middle of the chaos, confusion, and clutter, to enter into the gospel with those who know something about what it means to be excluded and exploited, unwanted and unvalued, labeled and left out, unable to move. When we read together and in community with those committed to breaking through barriers and structures, we begin to hear the gospel differently. This Gospel calls us together to get at the root, to transform, to upend the social divisions so that healing might happen, so that powers that confine and immobilize are overcome.

Mark 2 invites us into a radical discipleship that is communal as well as individual. Biblically there is no such thing as solo discipleship; there are no lone-ranger disciples. Even Jesus calls folks into community before beginning his public ministry. Jesus calls people into community to work, pray, and learn together. He calls us together to be there for and with each other in the good times and the hard times. And when Jesus sends the disciples out, he sends them two by two.

Discipleship in Jesus' name calls us into community to work together, collectively. Mark 2:3 shows us a picture of a radical collective of faith in action. A group unable to reach Jesus through a business-as-usual entry through the door brings a man to him, instead, through the roof. "Then some people came," the verse reads, "bringing to [Jesus] a paralyzed man, carried by four of them." A crowd brings this man to Jesus. Four of them are doing the hard work of carrying him, but others are with them in this faithful action. There's no way one person or even two could have carried the man to this house. Discipleship, the verse teaches us, requires creative communal collaboration.

The method of participatory Bible study asks us to imagine ourselves up against the problems posed in the Bible in community, in partnership, in real time. Imagine being recruited to the group of people carrying and accompanying this paralyzed man to Jesus. Some of us might have asked for information about what he has done to help himself: Is he active in our church? Do we have any evidence of his faith? Has he tried to pull himself up by his own bootstraps? Or maybe we might have recommended forming a committee—after all, only four people are needed to carry the man.

But even if we managed to become part of the crew accompanying and carrying the man to Jesus, most of us would have been deterred by the crowds. Surely someone would have noted that it's only common sense to wait until a later time; we need to turn back, there are just too many people and no way in through the door.

But, if we did stay and did try to figure out how to get the man to Jesus, imagine the conversation when someone says, "Look, we've got to go up on the roof. The only way in is to climb up on the roof of this house, cut a hole in this roof, dig all the way through the roof, and then lower him down to Jesus."

Someone would surely argue, "Oh no. Hold everything. There are policies and procedures!" or, "Structural change requires a planning committee," or, "We understand the need but we're going to have to apply for a permit," or, "There are building codes to be reckoned with. You can't just go digging through someone else's roof without permission."

Others might chime in, "We're likely to be arrested for destruction of property, not to mention trespassing, creating a public nuisance," and, "It's inappropriate. Here we are trying to win folks to Jesus, and you're going to alienate and upset folks. Surely there's another way," and the chorus: "We just have to wait. We have to find a method acceptable to everyone without causing conflict or creating problems."

We who are disciples are all too often tied up telling God and other folks what's appropriate and inappropriate, possible and impossible, acceptable and not acceptable. But putting ourselves in this story in community lets us hear ourselves, our proprieties, our fears, our reservations of rocking boats anew. Putting ourselves in the story as co-creators of the Living Word lets us wrestle with and toward the discipleship Jesus calls us to. Participating together in the story of the gospel can let us see and feel for ourselves that radical discipleship in the Bible is not about fitting in, making folks comfortable, or keeping things the way they are.

Radical discipleship calls us into community to defy the way things are for the sake of each other and for the sake of the kin-dom that God is already bringing about. The kin-dom of God is at hand!

In community and in the community of the gospel we see there is no time for accommodation or for patient waiting with some vague hope that the systems of exclusion will change over time.

"When Jesus saw their faith," reports Mark 2:5, "he said to the paralytic, 'Son, your sins are forgiven.'" "Their faith"—this was not the faith of the man on the mat that Jesus noted, but the faith of the rule-breaking intruders who dug through the roof in the middle of Jesus' standing-room-only gathering—is something to be *seen*. I'm suddenly struck by this radical definition of faith; here, faith is not an idea or confession, not simply a belief or creed, but something we can see, we can witness.

Faith in Mark is not about doctrine or right belief. It is not about attendance at Sunday school or church membership. Faith in the Gospel of Mark is made visible by the crew digging through the roof in this story; it's what the bleeding woman embodies when she pushes through the crowd to touch Jesus' cloak (5:25–34); it's the Syrophoenician woman confronting Jesus, refusing to be silenced or dismissed (7:28). Faith in the Gospel is the father who persists in seeking healing for his son (9:14–29), it's Bartimaeus hollering in the streets in defiance of those who ordered him to be quiet (10:46–52), it's what Jesus says the named male disciples don't yet have (4:40) and must have (11:22).

Just like this crew carrying the paralytic, the Syrophoenician woman's faith breaks through the theologies and structures of cultural norms and expectations (Mark 7:24–30). She defies established customs, upsets religious and societal boundaries, and in doing so she dismantles the structures that prevent healing from happening. This woman asks Jesus to heal her child. The disciples try to send her away. At first, Jesus ignores her and then he hurls a harsh dismissal at her, using language that implies her child is less worthy, less valued, less important than Jewish children. It is the harshest statement by Jesus recorded in the Gospels. Even so, this woman refuses to be dismissed, silenced, or belittled by Jesus. She confronts the narrowness of Jesus' theology and uses his language of oppression to come right back at him. She is, by writer and activist Alice Walker's definition, a "womanist . . . a feminist of color . . . usually referring to outrageous, audacious, courageous or willful behavior."[4] Jesus is utterly changed, liberated, by his encounter with this woman. It is a shock that we have this story in two of the Gospels and an even greater shock that so many churches, unlike Jesus, remain unchallenged and unchanged by this woman's fierce and fiery faith.

The woman is not Jewish, she is in fact a member of a distinctly different people. She is Greek, Syrophoenician, or according to Matthew, a Canaanite. She is outside the covenant community, and more, a woman, with no standing or power. She has no male human being with her and therefore has no permission to speak in public—let alone enter a house of strange men. This is a clash of cultures and religions, genders and status; this is a scandal then and now.

Many of the contemporary sermons on this text argue that Jesus was simply testing the woman's faith, teaching the male disciples what it means to cling to faith in spite of the barriers. If you engage in the participatory Bible study process with this text, the group representing the disciples will often come to this same conclusion. Indeed, those representing Jesus often fail to attend to the radicality of this story, arguing that Jesus was inviting her to show her faith, not meaning to be dismissive or disparaging. Surely, the Jesus we know would not say anything so hurtful; he would never have uttered these harsh words.

But those in the group taking on the role and social location of this woman will most often refuse to be silenced by polite explanations for Jesus' rudeness. They will, if they have spent time wrestling with what it felt like when these words were hurled at them, fire back. This group will note and call out the harsh, ugly, demeaning, xenophobic language Jesus uses. To be clear, Jesus is reflecting his culture, the norm of his day, repeating what must have been common language when talking about Gentiles, Syrophoenicians, Greeks, "others."

The Matthew version of this story (Matthew 15:21–28) makes the narrow theology even clearer for in Matthew, Jesus declares twice that he was sent not to Gentiles but only to the lost sheep of the house of Israel (Matthew 10:6, 15:24). Left un-interrogated, left without a participatory and communal engagement with this story, it becomes a theological justification for distance and disconnection, for "othering" and excluding.

But the group immersed in the story from the perspective of the woman will push, arguing that it was only because she would not quit, be sent away, or be ignored that Jesus continues the encounter. They will not accept the narrow theology that excludes their child. They do not believe that it is God's will for their daughter to continue to be tormented. They are convinced there's a wideness in God's mercy, that God's deepest desire is for the healing and wholeness of their child, and every child. In spite of the harsh rebuke, the racist language, the clear dismissal, this woman will not be silenced or sent away until her daughter is healed.

In the words of a male U.S. senator denouncing a female colleague he thought had gone too far, we see how familiar this faulty theological logic of dismissal can be. Responding to his colleague's demands he said, "She was warned. She was given an explanation. Nevertheless, she persisted."[5] So too, this woman in the Bible was "warned" and "given an explanation," but she refused to accept the injustice and she persisted. In doing so, she breaks Jesus open to a radically inclusive theology. In the United States, the words of warning recounted above, instead of silencing, turned into a rallying cry and a broader political engagement. The Gospel invites us to see how both women push back against warnings and rational explanations and in doing so, embody the kind of radical discipleship Jesus calls us into, how they both put flesh on their faith so that it can be seen. The Syrophoenician woman in the Bible invites Jesus to enlarge his theology and to create a table where no one waits for crumbs but all are welcomed to feast at the banquet table, to sit side by side.

Jesus, the fierce debater who silences other challengers, is changed by the encounter with this woman. His harsh *no* shifts into a resounding *yes* as he is confronted by the woman's faith and by her refusal to accept his theological justification for excluding her and her daughter from God's care and covenant. Mark has given us a story in which Jesus is converted by a woman from a different culture and faith—a story that is still hard for the church to hear. If Jesus can be changed by this woman, is it not also possible for the church to be converted, transformed, changed by those who are impoverished, by those who are crying out for healing and liberation, freedom and wholeness?

Elsa Tamez, biblical scholar, contextual theologian, and seminary professor in Costa Rica, emphasizes the importance of listening to the cries from, being immersed in the struggles of, and doing theology with those who are impoverished, oppressed, excluded, and persecuted argues,

> *The reading of the Bible from the perspective of impoverished and exploited peoples . . . has helped communities . . . to strengthen the hope that the situation of death can change because the God of the Bible is a God of justice, love and peace in solidarity with the poorest of the poor. . . . The understanding of the text comes out of the living context to give an answer to the challenges of the daily struggles and the global situation. It looks for the transformation of the reality that denies life.*[6]

Participating together in the story of this Syrophoenician woman challenges us to think about the ways in which the structures and theologies of church prevent us from really seeing and hearing those who are different. The story invites us to consider the power of our language to exclude and dismiss, the ways in which the patterns and practices of our congregations get in the way of healing happening, and to feel how those relationships are being created or restored. What structures and systems, assumptions and biases, theologies and ideologies prevent us from hearing the cries of women wailing for the healing of their children? What doctrine, dogma, traditions, and rituals prevent us from tearing through the structures so that those individuals, neighborhoods, and nations paralyzed by the powers of death can find healing and wholeness?

José Cárdenas Pallares, Mexican theologian, biblical scholar, and author of *A Poor Man Called Jesus*, writes that Mark "confronts us with a question: Whose side is God on? . . . What is at stake here is the acceptance either of a God who is on the side of human beings, especially human beings in need, or of a God whose back is turned on human pain."[7]

I think of a meditation that has haunted me over the years. I was in the middle of a move from one congregation to another and not quite happy with the decision. I spent time in prayerful meditation trying to center myself and prepare for the conflict that was surely coming. In this instance my meditation brought me to an image of a houseboat. Initially I panicked—I know nothing about houseboats. There seemed to be no one else around, the boat was not moving. I explored inside the boat, found the ignition but couldn't figure out how to start the houseboat let alone imagine myself driving it. I stewed, hoping to uncover some other person, some simple solution. And then suddenly it occurred to me: I'll just leave. I'm a strong swimmer. I'll just abandon the boat and swim to the nearest shore. "That's your problem, Janet," I thought. "You keep wanting to take everything with you. Abandon the boat and swim!" I was feeling quite pleased with my insight when I opened the curtains at the front of the houseboat and saw no land, only water, for as far as I could see.

The next time I meditated, the same image appeared. This time, I was standing on the back deck of the boat, staring out at the lifeless surroundings. The houseboat was stuck in the mud of the shore and for as far as I could see, there was no sign of life: no trees, no growing plants, no color, no people, no buildings, just this thick mud everywhere. And I couldn't walk on it or through it. I tried, but the mud sucked me deeper into itself and it was only after repeated attempts that I was able to pull myself back up on the deck of the boat. The meditation ended with me, caked with mud, sitting in despair on the deck. I decided the meditation was clearly meant for someone else—someone who knew more about boats and muck and getting through. Surely this one was not meant for me.

But the very next time I meditated, the image reappeared. I'm caked in mud, sitting on the deck, totally defeated. And then, all at once, it occurs to me that if I dismantle the boat, if I take it apart piece by piece, I can use the pieces to create a walkway on top of the mud. I cannot imagine where it will take me, or how tedious it will be to put down one plank and then come back for another and another, but I now begin to see the possibility for moving to some place where there might be signs of life.

Several days later, it occurs to me that this houseboat stuck in the mud and muck is a metaphor about the institutional church. So many of our patterns and practices, our rules and regulations, have landed us in the muck and we are stuck in a place with no life, unable to move. But if we take pieces, if we take scripture and our experiences, if we take reason and the traditions defined by Jesus, if we take faith we can see, we can move to a place of new life. Of course, that sounds much easier than it is—but in our practices of radical discipleship, can we begin to imagine tearing away whatever it is in our churches that gets in the way of healing happening?

Ched Myers, community organizer, popular educator, and theologian, notes that Jesus acts not just to bind up wounds, but to attack the structures that oppress and to confront theological narrowness. Walter Wink is a theologian who powerfully defined the domination systems and who wrote about and participated in militant nonviolence. These two biblical scholars write that healing in the Gospels is not simply the healing of individuals, but it is a public challenge to the theology and to the structures and systems that perpetuate exclusion and justify suffering. Healing, both in their reading and in a practice of radical discipleship, becomes a reordering of power and a restoring of right relationship in community.[8]

Brian Blount, an African-American seminary president and professor focusing on ethics and cultural studies, points out that in Mark, Jesus offers a radical reordering and opening of God's forgiveness. Blount writes, "Jesus provides an opening to God's forgiveness that need not detour through institutionalized provisions of the Temple cult and the religio-political leadership who maintain it."[9] So it is no wonder the scribes, the experts in both law and tradition, the scholars with interest in managing and maintaining the theological framework for those in power are offended, scandalized, and furious. Jesus upsets the social and religious order, defying norms by releasing this paralyzed man from any form of debt and reconnecting him with community, restoring his status as a full human being, when the religious authorities have labeled him as an outsider to be excluded from the covenant community.

For too long the church has behaved like the scribes in this story. While churches sing "Free to all, a healing stream" from the well-known hymn "Jesus, Keep Me Near the Cross," we often slam shut doors of hearts, minds, and buildings to those we label sinful. We become bogged down in theological debate instead of tearing through structures that prevent healing from happening, instead of restoring people to community, instead of celebrating God's liberating power and presence among us and joining those who are dancing in the streets.

But together, in a participatory Bible practice, let us imagine being the man on the mat, dependent on others to move. Surely he knew and trusted the community carrying him that day. Even so, imagine facing the crowd, seeing the multitude of barriers preventing you from entry into the house. Imagine being hoisted up onto the roof, witnessing the destruction of property, the clear intrusion into the home where Jesus was teaching.

Then imagine being lowered through the roof and becoming the center of attention, the focus of the angry debate between Jesus and the scribes. There, in front of everyone, Jesus announces your sins are forgiven and suddenly you become the focus as the religious authorities argue that Jesus has no authority to forgive sins and is guilty of blasphemy.

You are not even consulted. No one asks you a question; no one inquires about what's happening in your mind, body, and spirit. You become an object lesson caught in this theological debate. Through this story, we might ask how others see themselves in a similar predicament. Immigrants, migrants, people of color in the United States, those who are impoverished, young people struggling in the streets; those who are gay, lesbian, bisexual, transgender, queer, those locked in cages and those locked out of the church. As W.E.B. Du Bois writes in *The Souls of Black Folk*, "How does it feel to be a problem?"[10]

Maybe you went along with your friends hoping for a release from the paralysis, hoping for movement and liberation. Maybe, desperate as you must have been for agency, you went along with the rooftop invasion. But what must you have felt when Jesus suddenly announced that your sins had been forgiven?

It would have taken incredible courage for the man, in defiance of those in power and those in the community who are complicit with his exclusion, to take up his mat and walk. Perhaps those who carried him and those who accompanied the stretcher-bearers encouraged him as they walked alongside their friend, healed by God.

I thought of the importance of community in this story when I met a woman named Fayette. Fayette was living on the streets, struggling with mental illness and lupus, with poverty and racism. It was summer, hot and humid, and we had left the church door open during Bible study. Fayette must have heard our singing and she walked over towards the door and sat on the bottom step. When I saw her, I turned to invite her inside but before I could even get a word out, she stood up and walked away. But she started showing up with some regularity, arriving late and leaving early, always sitting on the steps, each time refusing to come inside. And then one day, she came inside.

Eventually, she began participating and sharing bits and pieces of her story. After a while, Fayette joined the class for people considering becoming new members and joining the church. She decided to be baptized. We talked about the meaning of baptism, noting the congregation's commitment to surround folks with a "community of love and forgiveness," and to live in such a way that we might remember who and whose we are: beloved, a precious child of God, beautiful to behold. In the class, we talked about the holy moment when we held black and brown children up before the congregation, and the congregation, adults who day after day were assaulted by white supremacy, adults who knew in their bodies, minds, and hearts the challenges facing black and brown children, together offered up our baptismal covenant, promising to live in such a way that this child, these children, these new members of our church family, would always know they are beloved, precious children of God and beautiful to behold.

This became Fayette's favorite part of the discussion and she would call us back to it again and again, asking, "And when I'm baptized, I am . . . ?" And everyone in the class soon learned to respond: "You are beloved, a precious child of God, and beautiful to behold." "Oh yes!" she'd exclaim and we'd go on to other topics until she brought it up again.

Then the day came. The choir was gathered around the pool singing, "Wade in the Water." Fayette went under, came spluttering up out of the icy cold water, drew in a new breath, looked all around and asked, "And now I am . . . ?" And everyone shouted, "You are beloved, a precious child of God, and beautiful to behold." "Oh, yes I am!" she declared and danced all around the fellowship hall.

Two months later I received a call at two in the morning. Fayette had been beaten and raped and was at the county hospital. So I went. As I was walking down the hall to her room, I could hear Fayette's voice. As I got closer, I saw her pacing back and forth, her hair sticking up everywhere, blood and tears marking her face, bruises already starting to show, her dress torn and dirty and buttoned all wrong. And then I heard her, "I am . . ." When I got to the door, she saw me, looked straight at me, and started once more saying, "I am beloved, a precious child of God, and . . ." At that moment, she caught sight of her reflection in the mirror, hesitated, turned back toward me and said, "I am beloved, a precious child of God, and . . . " Once more glancing at her reflection in the mirror, she continued, "and God is still working on me. If you come back tomorrow, I'll be so beautiful I'll take your breath away!"[11]

We are called to work together persistently, passionately, creatively, courageously. We are called to be willing to take risks and be outrageous so that new channels of healing might be opened. When we are truly convinced that this one called Jesus really is the one who restores brokenness to wholeness, when we know something about the balm in Gilead, about this one who brings liberation and hope, we will dig through any roof and do whatever it takes to break through all that stands in the way of healing. When we are truly called by Jesus into radical discipleship, it won't matter if folks want to argue it's inappropriate, that it's not a part of our tradition or custom, it's not the way we've always done things. It won't matter if it causes controversy or conflict. When we know the power of community and hear the cries of those hurting, we will come together and be willing to be outrageous in order to create new openings for healing.

We have already seen this kind of faith, this kind of radical discipleship in our world. I think of Nobel Peace Prize recipient Leymah Gbowee in Liberia and her vision of women praying together. Hers is a vision that took on flesh and forged a women's national nonviolent direct-action organizing movement, disrupted a nation defined by colonialism and violence, and forged new possibilities for democracy and peace. Thousands of women—old and young, Christian and Muslim, city dwellers and those from rural villages, grandmothers and teenagers, those living in poverty and those in economically comfortable households—made visible their trust in a God already at work to break through the stranglehold of the warlords and violence, patriarchy and sexism, greed and power brokering. It was the courage of these thousands of women making their outrageous faith visible that allowed them to restructure the first nation in Africa to democratically elect a woman as president.

As Leymah Gbowee comments in the film *Pray the Devil Back to Hell*, she was "looking at a people who had lost everything and still had hope."[12] We might substitute the word "faith" in place of "hope" in her comment—people who refused to give up, trusting that peace was still possible, that the structures and systems of death could be transformed through their embodied witness.

We have seen this faith, this radical discipleship, in the nonviolent anti-apartheid movement in South Africa. A prisoner of twenty-seven years became the president and the first official act of this new government was to abolish the death penalty. In a constitution written collaboratively with freedom seekers from around the world, South Africa spelled out human rights for all peoples in the nation, including those who are gay, lesbian, bisexual, transgender, queer. I remember seeing South African apartheid for the first time in 1978 and hoping that my children would live to see a free South Africa. I never anticipated that I would dance in the streets with those who tore through the structures and systems, the institutions and theologies that perpetuated the death and destruction by apartheid.

The Kairos Document, a theological statement issued in 1985 by a group of mainly black South African theologians, notes that it was not that churches had not articulated some good and strong demands for justice before the movement. It was rather that the justice called for was merely a . . .

> *justice of reform, that is to say, a justice that is determined by the oppressor, by the white minority, and that is offered to the people as a kind of concession . . . At the heart of this approach is the reliance upon "individual conversions" in response to "moralizing demands" to change the structures of a society . . . The present crisis with all its cruelty, brutality, and callousness is ample proof*

> *of the ineffectiveness of years and years of Christian "moralizing" about the need for love. The problem that we are dealing with here in South Africa is not merely a problem of personal guilt, it is a problem of structural injustice.*[13]

I remember this nation, the United States, paralyzed by racism and unwilling to move. And I remember a community of people coming together to carry this paralyzed nation to a place where truth telling and healing might begin. I remember ordinary citizens moving into the streets while folks on the sidelines screamed "too much, too soon" and worked to criminalize the nonviolent movement. I remember so many communities that dug through the structures and theologies of racism so that healing might happen. I remember communities facing dogs and hoses, sitting down at lunch counters and buses, standing up in marches and protests, singing songs of salvation, when they might have otherwise been silenced by sorrow and struggle. We have seen people who came together in a passionate, never-gonna-give-it-up, risk-taking, death-defying, life-giving, world-transforming radical discipleship.

We have seen this kind of discipleship in the Movement for Black Lives as thousands of people all over this nation joined a movement shaped by black women to "embody and practice justice, liberation and peace." Young and old, black and brown, queer and heterosexual, pastors and those who had never been in a church took to the streets to challenge state violence, the repeated murders by police of mostly young, mostly unarmed, black and brown human beings, awakening a nation, exposing the lies and trumpeting the truth in ways that could not be silenced.[14]

We are seeing it today: in the Moral Monday movement, in the revival of a Poor People's Campaign, in Standing Rock, in sanctuary and freedom movements, and the ongoing and just-being-born struggles for economic and racial justice, for housing and land equity. We are living through another time of prophetic and powerful people-led disruptions to business-as-usual, to language-as-pacifier, to death-dealing slowing down of folks on the sidelines saying "too much, too soon," to the silence and complacency of the church.

We are called into a radical discipleship that tears through the structures that get in the way of healing happening, including structures and policies in the church that maintain narrow theology, exclusionary policies and practices. Reconciling Ministries and Affirmation dig through the layers of church policy and practices that exclude those who are gay, lesbian, bisexual, transgender, queer. And though twelve-step programs may be common in congregations now, it has only been in recent years that the church has opened its doors and hearts to those struggling with addiction. My youngest brother was paralyzed by an addiction to drugs and alcohol, and by all the violence that accompanies this struggle. Thirty-some years ago, many churches would not allow Narcotics Anonymous or Alcoholics Anonymous groups to meet in our buildings—or if we did, they were allocated to basements and late-night meeting times. Many church folks responded to pleas for help with the comment that "you clean yourself up first, and then we'll see what might be possible," or "We'll add you to the prayer list." But it was the persistent, creative, aggressive people in twelve-step programs who carried my brother—and so many others—when he could not walk, who moved him from a place where he lay wasting away to a place where wholeness was restored, where he could believe he was a child of God, where he could get up and walk.

In a world where so many are paralyzed by forces that diminish life—powerful in so many nations, churches, neighborhoods, and individuals—we are urgently called to a radical discipleship that brings folks together. We are called to be creative, aggressive, persistent, passionate, and sometimes outrageous disciples. We are called to open up new possibilities for healing in Jesus' name.

Personal Reflection: Wrestling with Radical Discipleship

It's four in the morning in Nicaragua and I am standing on the corner waiting for an ecumenical community development truck to pick me up and take me into the mountains. I want to learn more about the work they do and how they manage to negotiate with the U.S.-funded and -supported Contra soldiers to move through their military-held territories into other mountain regions. The truck arrives and I jump into the back, joining several workers. They greet me with warm smiles and laughter, warning me that the trip will take hours and will be bumpy as we navigate dirt roads with rain-gullied holes. They are right: when we finally arrive at the tiny mountain village, we can hardly walk. It has started to rain and we are damp and chilled. The workers tell me we will now go from house to house to sit with the people of the village—and we do. In each house, we introduce ourselves, share stories, drink coffee, and listen to the struggles and hopes of the families. After we have completed the circuit, everyone gathers around a bare spot near the edge of the mountain. It is still raining and I cannot figure out why we are outside just standing, staring, waiting. One person after the other begins to talk about their plans to dig a well and the community development workers' willingness to work with them on their project. They decide on a timeline, list the equipment and workers needed, and then close the discussion with images of what life will be like in this village once they have easy access to safe drinking water.

Riding back in the truck, I try to find a polite way to ask why didn't you just go up there and dig a well? Why this incredible waste of time talking, drinking coffee, standing in the rain? This is so inefficient. In my country, we would have sent two people up to that village, the well would already be dug, and we'd be back home, warm, and rested. What I ask instead is, "Why was it important to spend so much time listening and talking in the rain? Couldn't you have sent a couple of workers up there to dig the well and have the entire project done by now?"

The workers looked incredulous and then burst into laughter. "Then who would care for the well? If it only belonged to the workers from the city, workers who came and went, who would make sure the well remained working?" It took me awhile but I finally caught on—people imagining, planning, and working to bring the well into reality were people who had ownership, responsibility, and investment in keeping the well working; the process was as important, maybe more important, than the product. This was community organizing at its best and it was radically different from the measures of "efficiency" and "effectiveness" in the United States.

For too long, I had thought about discipleship as simply individual and personal, rather than as something personal and communal and public. In this chapter, I listed some examples of where I have seen communal, public, and radical discipleship. In your journal reflection for this chapter, be as specific and concrete as possible as you respond to the following questions: Where have you seen this kind of faith? What might communal, collective, collaborative discipleship look like in your life? In your church and community?

NOTES

ENDNOTES

1. Oscar Romero, *The Violence of Love: The Pastoral Wisdom of Archbishop Oscar Romero*, compiled and translated by James Brockman (San Francisco: Harper & Row, Publishers, 1988), 28.

2. Romero, 197.

3. Lee Camp, *Mere Discipleship: Radical Christianity in a Rebellious World* (Grand Rapids, MI: Brazos Press, 2003), 24.

4. Alice Walker, *In Search of Our Mothers' Gardens* (San Diego: Harcourt Brace Jovanovich, 1983), xi.

5. Amy B. Wang, "'Nevertheless, she persisted' becomes new battle cry after McConnell silences Elizabeth Warren," *The Washington Post*, February 8, 2017, washingtonpost.com/news/the-fix/wp/2017/02/08/nevertheless-she-persisted-becomes-new-battle-cry-after-mcconnell-silences-elizabeth-warren/?utm_term=.815d7cfc102d.

6. Elsa Tamez, "The Bible and the Five Hundred Years of Conquest," in *God's Economy*, eds. Ross Kinsler and Gloria Kinsler, 9–10.

7. José Cárdenas Pallares, *A Poor Man Called Jesus: Reflections on the Gospel of Mark*, trans. Robert Barr (Maryknoll, NY: Orbis Books, 1982), 8.

8. Ched Myers, Joseph Nangle, Cynthia Moe-Lobeda, et. al. *"Say to This Mountain": Mark's Story of Discipleship* (Maryknoll, NY: Orbis Books, 1996), 14.

9. Brian Blount, *Go Preach! Mark's Kingdom Message and the Black Church Today* (Maryknoll, NY: Orbis Books, 1998), 80.

10. W.E.B. Du Bois, *The Souls of Black Folk* (New York: New American Library, 1969), 45.

11. A version of this story was published earlier: Janet Wolf, "Chosen for . . . " in *The Upper Room Disciplines, 1999* (Nashville: Upper Room Books, 1998), 128.

12. "Pray the Devil Back to Hell," Fork Films, accessed September 11, 2017, forkfilms.net/pray-the-devil-back-to-hell.

13. Willis Logan, ed., *The Kairos Covenant: Standing with South African Christians* (New York: Friendship Press, 1988), 19.

14. "Every day, we recommit to healing ourselves and each other, and to co-creating . . . a culture where each person feels seen, heard, and supported. We acknowledge, respect and celebrate differences and commonalities. We work vigorously for freedom and justice for Black people, and, by extension, all people. We intentionally build and nurture beloved community that is bonded together through a beautiful struggle that is restorative, not depleting . . . We embody and practice justice, liberation, and peace in our engagements with one another." See website blacklivesmatter.com/about/what-we-believe, accessed September 12, 2017.

Chapter 2

Engaging the Powers: Mark 5:1–20

This is the crime of which I accuse my country and my countrymen and for which neither I nor time nor history will ever forgive them, that they have destroyed and are destroying hundreds of thousands of lives and do not know it and do not want to know it.
—James Baldwin[1]

It is very easy to be servants of the word without disturbing the world: a very spiritualistic word, a word without any commitment to history, a word that can sound in any part of the world because it belongs to no part of the world. A word like that creates no problems, starts no conflicts. What starts conflicts and persecutions, what marks the genuine church, is when the word, burning like the word of the prophets, proclaims to the people and accuses: proclaims God's wonders . . . and accuses of sin those who oppose God's reign, so that they may tear that sin out of their hearts, out of their societies, out of their laws—out of the structures that oppress, that imprison, that violate the rights of God and humanity. This is the hard service of the word.
—Oscar Romero, December 10, 1977[2]

We're sitting in a circle of rickety chairs on the stage of a seminary's fellowship hall and the room is filled with the sweet smells of good food: roasted chicken, grilled salmon with dill, tangy citrus fruit, and a deep, dark chocolate cake. We are trying to hear each other but it is not easy—there are still folks lingering over lunches, students passing through to get to class, and the sounds of pans clanging and of caterers cleaning up. We pull in closer to each other, wondering if this is going to be worth anyone's time. About twenty organizers and activists, seminary students and professors, community folks and pastors are gathering for a one-and-a-half-hour workshop on redefining prison ministry as part of a national conference on immigration and incarceration. We're already running fifteen minutes late, and folks are still sliding into the circle.

Leroy opens the workshop by asking people to offer their names—no titles—just the name they want to be called, and why they have come into this circle. For most, the topic and the experience of imprisonization are new but they might be interested in prison ministry. "You know," the participants say, "visiting those folks who are locked up, maybe helping them out a bit." Most will say that they don't know a lot about prisons, and it is somewhat scary to imagine going inside one, but they think maybe they should so they want to know more.

Leroy surprises those gathered by saying that he is one of the many who have been caged. He was one of the speakers the night before, holding his own with academics and activists, with theologians and seminary students, and now he begins to crumble the stereotypes about who is in prison and why by identifying himself as one who has been caged. Leroy tells the circle he is one of the 6 million people who have lost their right to vote because they have a felony conviction, and that he is less than a year removed from being one of the 2.3 million people in this country living in cages.[3] He shares a bit of his story, including the consequences of being criminalized at an early age, the difficulties of growing up in prison, and of reentering a world in which he had never driven a car, never held a cell phone, never used an ATM, never ordered in a restaurant, never paid a bill, or owned anything other than his clothes and a used bike. And then we invite the participants into a biblical text about Jesus' arrival to a place of exile. I begin:

> *Forget any sermons you have heard on Mark 5:1–20, any commentaries or Bible studies. For twenty minutes, immerse yourself in the story, and imagine you are either the man who was possessed or Legion; either the pig herders and townspeople, or Jesus. Instead of trying to explain or interpret the story,*

> *ask, from the viewpoint of your location in the story, why you do what you do. What brings you hope and what provokes fear? What is happening in your head and your heart as this story unfolds? Everyone has to be some place in the story. There are no bystanders.*

Leroy continues:

> *If you are in the small group identified as the man who was possessed, ask yourself what it feels like to be chained, to break the shackles only to have them replaced over and over again; to know the townspeople must hear you howling and yet abandon you to exile? What does it feel like when Legion speaks for you, when you have no voice to offer up your own version of your story? What does it feel like to be "clothed and in [your] right mind" and have people still be afraid of you? How do you feel when Jesus sends you back to the very community that exiled you? What does it mean to you that this text is most often referred to as the story of the "Gerasene demoniac," even though you are no longer possessed?*

Only after the small groups listen to the story from their particular perspective—not attempting to explain anyone else's behavior, only focusing on the story's impact on them—do they begin to explore the question that invites them and their world in: "So what?" Great story, but where does it sing to our souls with enough power to move us in new directions? Where does it challenge us? Where and how does it frighten us? What might it look like when it takes on flesh in our home territory? Leroy pulled out his parole card—a photo ID with large red letters that identified him as a parolee under the jurisdiction of the Tennessee Department of Corrections—and his pass papers, the document that allows him to travel to this national conference. Leroy comments:

> *See this piece of paper? This paper says I belong to the state of Tennessee, that if I am ever found without this paper and this identification card from the Tennessee Department of Corrections, I am subject to immediate arrest and imprisonment. Not because of anything I do, not because I broke some law, but just because after seventeen years of being locked up and one year being out, I still belong to the prison system in Tennessee.*

The identification card and travel pass remind folks of the passes black and brown South Africans were required to carry during apartheid. And of Jim Crow laws. And of Legion in this story, the powers that occupy, inhabit, possess, and diminish individuals, communities, and nations.

The impact of Leroy's presence and leadership in this discussion is crucial—he makes visible the effect of social location, the limitations of theology that is disconnected from those who are struggling, pushed to the edge. His presence underlines the importance of doing theology in partnership with those who have been or are now caged by our prison-industrial complex.

At the end of the workshop, Leroy asks people to once again offer their names and then a gift they will take with them from this time together. One New Testament scholar and professor in the circle says she is both elated at the power of the method to ignite a new way of seeing and being, and sad that while she teaches liberation theology and biblical study from the bottom up, she could not have provoked in a semester what this method has accomplished in roughly one hour.

A graduate theology student who passed the first time around ends our closing circle by saying that he had given up on the Bible but now saw the radical claims of the texts and the ways in which scripture has been taken from the people to be used as a form of control. He wants to take the Bible back. He wants to lift up the Jesus he encountered because of Leroy; the Jesus who was a prisoner removed from his community, criminalized, tried and convicted by the government, incarcerated, battered, tortured, and executed in a state-sanctioned murder.[4]

How is it that most churches are disconnected from those caged in jails and prisons? And how does that shrink our understanding of God and our world? All too often, congregations engaged in prison ministry define their work through the lens of charity instead of justice. What might it mean to redefine prison ministry as not only accompanying and supporting people who are incarcerated and those who are returning citizens, but also working to challenge and change the theologies, systems, and structures that have labeled people as disposable in the first place? How might partnership with those who have been criminalized redefine the churches' understandings of children's ministry, youth ministry, prison ministry, evangelism, and Christian education?

Like so many other Gospel stories, Mark 5 is an invitation to uncover the ways in which we smooth the rough edges and sharp corners of the Gospel. It is an invitation to uncover how we downsize and domesticate the stories so that they fit in with what is, instead of allowing the stories to disrupt and disturb all that is for the sake of what God is already bringing about. The text is a reminder that the Gospel is intended to startle us and awaken us. It is meant to confront us with the ways we have compromised with the powers that be, defying this Jesus who keeps showing up in places where he is not welcome, who refuses to leave even when the demons, the evil powers, and then the townspeople beg him to do so. Mark 5 demands that we own up to the times when we would defy this Jesus who exposes what other folks mean to keep hidden; who includes, affirms, and liberates folks whom others have gone to great lengths to exclude, silence, dismiss, and permanently disenfranchise.

The man is said to be at home among the tombs; he is chained, shackled, struggling, howling, and raging against all efforts to contain him. He is tortured, exiled from the community. He is discarded, labeled expendable, rendered disposable. The townspeople and pig herders do not seem to see or hear this man, but Mark wants to make sure her readers are confronted, exposed, and provoked to respond.

Consistently the gospel begins here, in just such a place as this cemetery, reminding us that our social location matters—where we are, who we listen to and learn from shapes our hearing of and response to the gospel. The pig herders and townspeople beg Jesus to leave, but the man, now clothed and in his right mind, begs to be allowed to accompany Jesus. Location matters, and the struggle for so many of our congregations is our proximity to and alliances with power and our distance from those individuals and communities that are occupied, possessed, tormented.

Jesus steps out of the boat and into the cemetery (Mark 5:2–3). By Chapter 3 in Mark, Jesus has already upset and alienated the religious authorities, his family has come to restrain him (3:21), the scribes have accused him of being possessed (3:30), and the Pharisees have conspired with the Herodians on "how to destroy him" (3:6). Now, here in Chapter 5, Jesus moves into a new area; he moves into Gentile territory. In this new land, he does not go to meet with religious authorities or local congregations, he makes no appointments with those in political power or business leaders, and he attends no chamber of commerce or seminary luncheons. Jesus goes straight to the place of death, the place where Legion, the multitude of dominating powers, occupies and possesses human beings and communities.

Sit with the man in this story for a moment and ask what powers occupy our communities, our nation, in ways that exile and exclude, that demonize and dehumanize. Think of all the individuals, neighborhoods, communities, and nations that are occupied—possessed by the powers, structures, and systems of racism and poverty, by militarism and economic exploitation, by the prison-industrial complex, and by a health care system that deals in death. Think of all the abuse and battering, illness and addiction, depression and despair. Think of folks working two jobs and still not able to pay their bills. Think of single mamas so tired and lonely that they ache for someone to hold them gently for just a moment. Folks working long, hard hours and then watching others they trained getting higher salaries and larger promotions. Families living in a world where racism and poverty are so fierce, joining the military becomes the only real option for children to get a higher education and then these children—not the children of the president or the children of cabinet members or Congress, not the children of the wealthy, powerful, and privileged—but your child is sent to the front lines of a war you did not choose and do not want. And on top of it all, so many churches are silent at best and complicit at worst with the very systems that destroy and diminish life.

Jesus goes straight to the place of death, the place where we do not expect to find him. The townspeople must have heard the man wailing. Someone must have taken the food to the cemetery and replaced the chains. In Mark 5, Jesus goes to the cemetery, a reminder that we are called to do theology from the margins—listen to, learn from, be identified with, stand side by side with those who are struggling hard just to get by.

Walter Wink argues that Gospel healings are never simply individual healings but public challenges to narrow theologies and oppressive systems.[5] And Ched Myers notes that in the Gospel healings, Jesus shifts the scandal from people labeled unclean to the systems, structures, and theologies that are unclean.[6]

Mark's story shifts the scandal to public challenges that most often upset the surrounding communities: the scandal is not the man who is possessed in Mark 1:21–24, but the powers that diminish life and the community that refuses to intervene. The scandal is not the man on the mat or the crew who digs through the roof in Mark 2:1–12, but the religious authorities who value power and authority over healing and wholeness. The scandal is not the man with a withered hand in Mark 3:1–6, but the Pharisees whose hard hearts narrow their definition of the Sabbath. The scandal is not the bleeding woman who touches Jesus' clothing in Mark 5:24–34, but those whose theology labeled her unclean and unwanted. The scandal is not the Syrophoenician woman insisting on the healing of her daughter in Mark 7:24–30, but the male disciples whose narrow theology excludes so many of God's children. The scandal is not Bartimaeus hollering in the streets in Mark 10:46–52, but those who sought to silence him; the scandal is not the woman who anoints Jesus in Mark

14:3–9, but the male disciples who seek to discount and discredit her and a church that continues to miss the heart of the story.

The scandal is not the man who is possessed but the town that exiled him in the first place. The scandal is the theology required to render some folks disposable, expendable. It is the systems that kept his imprisonization in place, replacing chains and shackles over and over again in an attempt to keep him locked up and locked out. And the scandal is the church that still refers to the man as the "Gerasene demoniac," an old label that no longer applies.

The scandal is not individual children who are failing in school, but the systematic resegregation of our public schools by race and class. It is the structures and systems that occupy and possess our communities, and relentlessly push black and brown and impoverished children from the cradle into jail cells and prisons.

The scandal is not the behavior of Trayvon Martin or Jordan Davis, not the behavior of Michael Brown, Yvette Smith, or Eric Garner, not the behavior of Ezell Ford, Aiyana Stanley-Jones, John Crawford, VonDerrit Myers, Tamir Rice, Tanisha Anderson, Walter Scott, Freddie Gray, Shereese Francis, Kalief Browder, Miriam Carey, Philandro Castile, Oscar Grant, Rekia Boyd, and so many others. The scandal is police forces that have been trained as soldiers, given military equipment, and turned into occupying forces in communities of color; the scandal is the criminalization of black and brown bodies.[7]

The scandal is churches and seminaries that are silent, complacent, complicit with the systems of institutional racialized violence. The scandal is those of us who become theological justifiers for the structures of oppression.

The scandal is not people inside jails and prisons, but a nation that has less than 5 percent of the world's population warehousing more than 25 percent of the world's prisoners. According to Michelle Alexander, civil rights lawyer and author of *The New Jim Crow: Mass Incarceration in the Age of Colorblindness*, more African Americans are under correctional control today—in prison or jail, on probation or parole—than were enslaved in 1850; more black men are disenfranchised today than in 1870.[8] Susan Burton, a formerly caged organizer, founder of A New Life Reentry Program, writes, "Most women in U.S. prisons were, first, victims. It's estimated that eighty-five percent of locked-up women were, at some or many points in their lives, physically or sexually abused, or both. Disproportionately, these women are black and poor. I was born and raised in those statistics . . . In the U.S., up to one hundred million people have a criminal record—that's one in three Americans."[9] This is the scandal.

When we view the scandal as the folks who are incarcerated, we often end up with prison ministry that focuses on the good church people from the outside fixing up and saving the bad people on the inside. But when we shift the scandal in radical discipleship, we are called instead to challenge an unjust structure that is systematically devastating families and communities of color, especially those who are impoverished.

Jesus shifts the scandal from people labeled unclean to the theologies that distance and dismiss, to the structures that diminish and deny. The scandal is not the sixteen thousand people who are released from prison every month in this country, most labeled as a convicted felon, a label that becomes a permanent consignment to occupation and possession by the prison-industrial complex. The scandal is the churches and communities who collaborate with powers of domination to consistently exclude, condemn, and make integration into community all but impossible.

The scandal is not folks labeled illegal aliens—no human being is illegal. The scandal is a country that has stolen land from Mexico and propped up an economic system that requires cheap labor. It is clergy who have settled in, as Walter Wink notes, as "kept chaplains of an unjust order."[10]

The scandal is not people who are gay, lesbian, bisexual, transgender, queer. The scandal is a church that is called to be known by our love, theologically justifying the exclusion and continued discrimination, the bigotry and hatred of homophobia and heterosexism.

In the beginning of this story, the man who is occupied has been labeled unclean, unworthy, unwanted, unimportant. But by the end, he has been restored to wholeness and is sent back into the community to tell the story of God's goodness. For many of us, the text offers echoes of our own experiences. In story after story, including our own, we discover a God who frees our tongues, gives us language and a new name, a God who liberates us from occupation and sends us back to tell our story. We discover in Jesus the truth about who we are in defiance of all the names the systems give us—we are God's somebodies, awesomely and wondrously made as Psalm 139 says. Gospel healings are never simply individual healings but public challenges to narrow theology and oppressive systems. They are a shifting of the scandal from unclean people to unclean powers and principalities, systems and structures, theologies and institutions.

Disciples are called to shape their lives by following Jesus, this one who repeatedly engages powers and principalities. Silence, denial, distance, or refusal to recognize and engage power is not optional for disciples of Jesus, at least not according to the Gospel texts. In Mark 5:8, Jesus orders Legion to come out of the man. This confrontation with forces that diminish life is part of our job description as disciples. In Chapter 6 of Mark, disciples have three tasks: to proclaim the gospel good news that "the kin-dom of God is at hand!"; to heal those who are wounded and suffering; and to cast out demons, the powers and principalities of death.

William Stringfellow, an Episcopalian lay theologian and lawyer working in Harlem, wrote and spoke about powers and principalities, reminding people that the phrase is fundamentally biblical: "For we wrestle not against flesh and blood, but against principalities, against powers" (Ephesians 6:12; King James Version). And yet, he notes, when he talked about powers and principalities in seminaries and congregations, folks looked at him as if he were speaking about something totally unrelated to their world. On the other hand, he argued, folks on the streets knew exactly what he was talking about. They know who the "man" or Legion is and how he operates, they know who is sucking up life out of the neighborhood, and they know who has the power to consign folks to places of death and destruction.

And people listening to Jesus would have recognized the reference immediately—some may have wanted to use it against him at his trial. The tenth Legion had been located in Palestine since 6 CE and had as its banner symbol a wild boar or pig. There were two thousand men in a Roman battalion, sometimes called legion. In this story the evil, unclean, occupying powers are forced out of the man and into the pigs who immediately rush over the cliff to be drowned in the sea, much like Pharaoh's army in Exodus 14. The reference is not subtle. According to A.J. Levine, Jewish theologian, New Testament scholar, and seminary professor, you might substitute Al Qaeda to wake folks up to the power of this image, or depending on your social location, the 101st Airborne.[11] This story is a direct assault on the Roman Empire; it is a clash of power between the Roman occupiers and the kingdom, kin-dom, of God. And it parallels the assault on the religious elite's control of the synagogue in Mark Chapter 1.

Radical discipleship calls us to engage powers and principalities, systems and structures that diminish life, and this work has never been more urgent or difficult. Theodore Jennings notes that the reign of God is not the reign of Caesar—any Caesar—even an enlightened Caesar. The way of love, he writes, is not the same as the way of domination and division. God's kin-dom inevitably clashes with economic and political systems. And the story is a reminder that the church is not an escape. It is not a safe haven where we go to avoid the world's problems. The church is the community that empowers us to wade into struggles in Jesus' name. It prepares us not simply for some heaven after we die but for confrontation with empire here and now. It equips us to uncover and unmask, to confront and challenge systems and structures of empire and domination in us and the world around us.

Bishop Minerva Carcaño, the first female Hispanic bishop in The United Methodist Church, consistently engages powers and principalities, initiating and sustaining action to challenge and change systems and structures, theologies and institutions. "Believing and seeing Jesus is about participating in God's incredible, great plan of saving the whole world from its sin, its misery and its self-inflicted pain."[12] Her testimony before a congressional subcommittee, "The Real Victims of a Reckless and Lawless Immigration Policy: Families and Survivors Speak Out on the Real Cost of This Administration's Policies," drew from the Social Principles in *The Book of Discipline of The United Methodist Church 2016* and expressed strong support for the ongoing sanctuary movement.[13] Carcaño persistently confronts public policies that diminish and harm, threaten and terrorize communities of immigrants, refugees, and impoverished peoples. Quoting words from a song by Selena, a slain Tex-Mex singer, Carcaño calls us to love: "If we all love each other the world will change . . . Tell me you're going to live today so that tomorrow is worthy of hope. If we all love each other the world will change."[14]

Carcaño embodies faith you can see, calling on all of us to allow "the words of others [to] enter our being, and go through our defenses and our fears."[15] She leads groups to walk along the border between the United States and Mexico so that with her they discover signs of the desperation and hardships of those crossing the border to flee violence and economic exploitation. Together, they find baby bottles, tiny shoes, a shattered rattle. She invites others to join her in serving communion through the wire of the border wall, remembering the boundary-breaking, wall-demolishing, liberating and reconciling Jesus. When she became the president of the Western Jurisdictional College of Bishops, Carcaño promised to "challenge statements and actions that offend, denigrate, or exclude any person because of the color of their skin, their economic circumstance, their political persuasion, their gender or their sexual orientation."[16] For so much of her work, what it means to challenge—what it means to engage the powers—is to, as a radical disciple, bring people together in proximity, in powerful prayerful proximity to the margins, in the death-dealing borders, in the cemeteries Jesus leads us toward, trusting in the power of love.

And Carcaño is not alone. Congregations and religious communities all over—in prison camps, on Syrian rafts in the Mediterranean Sea, in rust-belts-turned-opioid-belts, in Standing Rock—are engaging powers and creating prophetic radical discipleship circles and actions.

We can see this in United Methodist Women's work to end poverty, confront climate change, dismantle racism, register voters, support the rights of young girls around the world, and do justice in partnership with immigrants. United Methodist Women members in the United States have moved into the streets in partnership with others, and into the halls of legislatures and Congress to call for an end to the criminalization of communities of color. It was United Methodist Women that introduced and won re-adoption of the Charter for Racial Justice by the 2016 General Conference, emphasizing that "racism robs all human beings of their wholeness and is used as the justification for social, economic and political exploitation."[17]

In Ferguson, Missouri, after the killing of Michael Brown, several churches were pulled into the streets by young activists and, in that movement, they have found new life.[18] The pastors and lay leaders did not go as those who were in charge, but as those who wanted to learn more, those who had been broken open by the clear violation of life and yearned to be part of the healing. They opened their sanctuaries and their hearts, their minds and their lives, and joined with others in risking their safety and freedom to expose the lies of empire. The Rev. Traci Blackmon, Ferguson pastor and executive minister of Justice and Witness Ministries in the United Church of Christ, describes the Ferguson movement as a Pentecostal moment, a church born in the streets, a needed revolution, an awakening and rebirth. Churches, Blackmon declares, had become complicit in the bondage of our people, had bought in to that which is not of God. Blackmon argues that it was the young people who had left the church who helped pastors and parents, clergy and community find what it means to be the church of Jesus Christ again. Together, the young people who had left the church and the church people who had lost the church, were forged in the fires of Ferguson. Together, they reordered the world; they redefined what it means to be the church, pulling the church out of sanctuaries and silence and into the streets, and offering the chant, "Whose streets? Our streets!"[19] And this is the faith in Mark—the unwillingness to wait, the fierce urgency of leaning into expectancy and hope here and now, as glimpses of the kin-dom emerge.

The church is called to embody alternatives—to make visible the possibilities for healing and liberation. The man freed from Legion is sent back to tell the story of all that God is doing. His witness demonstrates that change is not only possible but happening, that occupying forces, as powerful as they are, will not have the last word, that we need not be defined or silenced by powers that seek to possess. We are to be God's contrast community. And, as Leroy explained to us that day as we read the Gospel together in the circle, not to take sides—to remain silent—is to side with those in power. There is no neutral position.

What might it mean to become partners in the change God is already bringing about, partners in liberating freedom movements that create visible alternatives to the existing systems of domination? What might Beloved Community look like in a time when so many people are investing in building walls instead of bridges? Mark's story pushes us to question the pig herders and townspeople, and to ask ourselves why is it that they are more afraid of and upset by the man who is now clothed and in his right mind than they were when he was being tortured? Are we among the crowd that is so upset by the upside down and right-side up gospel that we would rather have Jesus leave our neighborhood than reorder our systems of power?

Walter Brueggemann notes, "The narrative of the Exodus is designed to show the radical criticism and radical delegitimizing of the Egyptian empire . . . aimed at nothing less than the dismantling of the empire both in its social practices and in its mythic pretensions . . . Israel emerged . . . as a genuine alternative community."[20]

Susan Burton is the founder and executive director of A New Way of Life, a network of safe houses for women coming out of prison, a "genuine alternative community." In addition to her work focusing on safe houses, free legal clinics, advocacy campaigns, and legislative reform efforts, Susan is the creator of Women Organizing for Justice and Opportunity. This six-month intensive training program focuses on power analysis and political structures, community organizing and civic engagement, nonviolent human rights movements and methods and strategies aimed at empowering women to tell their stories, to facilitate meetings, and to assure health and wellness on a budget. In describing Susan's work, Michelle Alexander writes,

> There once lived a woman with deep brown skin and black hair who freed people from bondage and ushered them to safety. . . . This courageous soul knew well the fear and desperation of each one who came to her, seeing in their eyes all the pain she felt years ago when she had been abused and shackled and finally, began her own journey to freedom . . . A relentless advocate for justice, this woman was a proud abolitionist and freedom fighter. . . . Some people know this woman by the name Harriet Tubman. I know her as Susan.[21]

These righteous leaders, these prophetic communities are all around us. When congregations and communities sponsor Children's Defense Fund Freedom Schools, dismantle zero-tolerance policies, engage in restorative justice practices, facilitate mediation, become long-term partners with those who are caged to redefine prison ministry from the inside out, we too carry forward this freedom-fighting legacy, we too give flesh to what is possible and allow people to experience a genuine alternative. Against these powers and principalities—against these narrow and hateful words thrown at us from what sometimes feels like all sides, we are invited to be God's contrast community, God's demonstration plot, or, as author Anne Lamott says, to be "God's sign language in a world gone deaf." People are to look at us and see the alternative. As Peter Storey, former Methodist bishop of Southern Africa, anti-apartheid activist, seminary professor, and author, says, we are called to be God's visual aid.

Personal Reflection: Wrestling with Radical Discipleship

The Children's Defense Fund team I work with has designed a four-to-six-week series of participatory workshops with middle and high school youth to explore the cradle-to-prison pipeline. At the end of the series, the students are given a wooden desk, the same kind of desk we sit at inside the maximum security prison, and an orange jumpsuit, the uniform worn by people in jails across the country. They are invited to use the desk and jumpsuit—and any other materials they want—to create an art piece that makes visible what the cradle-to-prison pipeline looks like when it shows up in their lives.

One group of young people, meeting in a church across the street from the public housing project where they lived, bolted a Bible and handcuffs to the desk. The orange suit was shellacked so it was stiff, but lifeless, thin, empty, and propped up in the chair of the desk with shackles around the ankles. When asked to talk about their art project, the young people described the role of the church in excluding and criminalizing black and brown bodies, especially those of young people. They shared stories of the way in which the Bible had been used to lock them up and out—as a weapon of oppression rather than a resource for liberation and wholeness, healing and hope. Some of the church members were angry and shocked, outraged that the young people had drilled a hole through a Bible. Until one younger student asked them, "Are you not at least a little bit mad about these stories we've shared?" And another student added, "How can you be more upset about a book than all this hurt and harm, trauma and trouble that's happening, really?"

In the Mark story featured in this chapter, the townspeople and pig herders ask Jesus to leave, refusing to be transformed by their encounter with this liberating Jesus. Take some time before beginning the next chapter to reflect in your journal on what came up for you in this chapter. In what ways might you, your church, your community be more confronted than comforted by this story of a disruptive Jesus? How might the stories in this chapter assist you in initiating a justice-seeking, authentically-rooted-in-partnership prison ministry?

The Book of Discipline of The United Methodist Church 2016 outlines our commitment to restorative justice, in stark contrast to the retributive justice that currently defines our criminal justice system. Noting that restorative justice "grows out of biblical authority [and] emphasizes a right relationship with God, self, and community," *The Book of Discipline* goes on to say, "Through God's transforming power, restorative justice seeks to repair the damage, right the wrong, and bring healing to all involved. . . . The Church is transformed when it responds to the claims of discipleship by becoming an agent of healing and systemic change."[22] What might restorative justice restore for you, for your communities?

NOTES

ENDNOTES

1. James Baldwin, *The Fire Next Time* (New York: Dell Publishing Company, 1967), 15.

2. Oscar Romero, *The Violence of Love: The Pastoral Wisdom of Archbishop Oscar Romero*, compiled and translated by James Brockman (San Francisco: Harper & Row, Publishers, 1988), 20.

3. "Felony Disenfranchisement: A Primer," *The Sentencing Project*, accessed September 11, 2017, sentencingproject.org/doc/publications/fd_Felony%20Disenfranchisement%20Primer.pdf.

4. Mumia Abu-Jamal, *Death Blossoms: Reflections from a Prisoner of Conscience* (Brooklyn: Litmus Books, 1996), 39.

5. Walter Wink, *Engaging the Powers: Discernment and Resistance in a World of Domination* (Minneapolis: Fortress Press, 1992), 137.

6. Ched Myers, *Binding the Strong Man: A Political Reading of Mark's Story of Jesus* (Maryknoll, New York: Orbis Books, 1988), Chapter 4. See also, "Challenging the Status Quo: Jesus Contests Scribal Authority," Radical Discipleship, accessed August 8, 2017, radicaldiscipleship.net/2015/01/29/lets-catch-some-big-fish-jesus-call-to-discipleship-in-a-world-of-injustice-2.

7. Those listed are black and brown, many young, almost all killed by the police though they were unarmed—there are many more that could have been listed. I have listed Kalief Browder as being an unarmed teenager murdered by the police and the criminal justice system—he was arrested at age 16, charged with stealing a backpack. There was no trial or conviction and though he maintained his innocence, he was confined to prison at Rikers for three years, almost two of those in solitary. Kalief committed suicide after his release, unable to recuperate from the trauma, isolation, and repeated brutal beatings received at Rikers when he was a juvenile. Trayvon Martin, 17, February 26, 2012; Jordan Davis, 17, November 23, 2012; Michael Brown, 18, August 9, 2014; Yvette Smith, 47, February 16, 2014; Eric Garner, 43, July 17, 2014; Ezell Ford, 25, August 11, 2014; Aiyana Stanley-Jones, 7, May 16, 2010; John Crawford III, 22, August 5, 2014; Vonderrit Myers, 18, October 8, 2014; Tamir Rice, 12, November 23, 2014; Tanisha Anderson, 37, November 13, 2014; Walter Scott, 50, April 4, 2015; Freddie Gray, 25, April 12, 2015; Shereese Francis, 30, March 15, 2012; Kalief

Browder, 22, June 6, 2015; Miriam Carey, 34, October 3, 2013; Philando Castile, 32, July 6, 2016; Oscar Grant III, 22, January 1, 2009; Rekia Boyd, 22, March 21, 2012. And so many more.

8. Michelle Alexander, *The New Jim Crow: Mass Incarceration in the Age of Colorblindness* (New York: The New Press, 2012), 175.

9. Susan Burton and Cari Lynn, *Becoming Ms. Burton: From Prison to Recovery to Leading the Fight for Incarcerated Women* (New York: The New Press, 2017), dedication page.

10. Walter Wink, *Unmasking the Powers: The Invisible Forces That Determine Human Existence* (Minneapolis: Fortress Press, 2006), 137.

11. Amy-Jill Levine's comments on Mark 5 and the 101st Airborne were offered in her Bible study session during "Faith, Hope and Love" Reconciling Ministries Network Convocation, Nashville, August 2–5, 2007.

12. Minerva Carcaño, *I Believe in Jesus* (New York: Women's Division, The General Board of Global Ministries, The United Methodist Church, 2008), 96.

13. The sanctuary movement was started in the 1980s by John Fife, a Presbyterian pastor working with others to create a form of underground railroad and safe passage for refugees and immigrants from Central America that involved more than five hundred churches and synagogues. John Fife went on to found the Samaritan Patrol, groups of people walking the border areas to search for those in distress and danger, which has become the No More Deaths/No Mas Muertes movement, providing medical care for migrants crossing the desert. See forms.nomoredeaths.org/en.

14. Carcaño, 105.

15. Ibid., 67.

16. "Bishop Joins Colleagues at U.S.-Mexico Border," Western PA Conference, The United Methodist Church, News, May 18, 2013, wpaumc.org/newsdetail/49433.

17. *The Book of Resolutions of The United Methodist Church 2016* (Nashville: The United Methodist Publishing House, 2016), 3371.

ENDNOTES *continued*

18. Michael Brown, an unarmed black teenager, was shot and killed by a white police officer in Ferguson, Missouri, a suburb of St. Louis, on August 9, 2014; his body was left in the street for more than four hours. More information about his murder and the church's response can be found online at divinity.yale.edu/news/justice-work-and-gospel-conversation-traci-blackmon and sojo.net/articles/faith-action/blood-did-it-why-michael-browns-death-was-different.

19. Traci Blackmon, Presentation, Children's Defense Fund's Samuel DeWitt Proctor Child Advocacy Institute, July 19, 2017, Alex Haley Farm, Clinton, TN.

20. Walter Brueggemann, *The Prophetic Imagination*, second edition (Minneapolis: Fortress Press, 2001), 9.

21. Michelle Alexander, Foreword in *Becoming Ms. Burton*, by Susan Burton (New York: The New Press, 2017).

22. *The Book of Discipline of The United Methodist Church 2016* (Nashville: The United Methodist Publishing House, 2016), 140–141. See also United Methodist Women's resources on restorative justice, including Harmon Wray's *Restorative Justice: Moving Beyond Punishment* (New York: General Board of Global Ministries, The United Methodist Church, 2002).

Chapter 3

Liberation and Life: Thy Kin-dom Come! Mark 9:14–29

God's reign is already present on our earth . . . That is the hope that inspires Christians. We know that every effort to better society, especially when injustice and sin are so ingrained, is an effort that God blesses, that God wants, that God demands of us.
—Oscar Romero, March 24, 1980[1]

God's reign did not begin with Jesus. Jesus proclaimed it, made clear what it means, worked hard to bring about a new human community inspired by it. He disclosed what had already been present in the beginning of God's creation: all human beings are endowed with inviolable humanity . . . What follows from this is self-evident. The society that keeps the poor forever poor is opposed to the reign of God. A nation that discriminates against certain people because of the color of their skin contradicts the reign of God. The government that suppresses human rights, and arrests, tortures, imprisons, or murders political dissidents betrays the reign of God. The world that perpetuates patriarchal control over women is hostile to the reign of God. And the religious community that has no room for people of other religious communities is far from being the reign of God.
—C.S. Song, Jesus and the Reign of God[2]

The kingdom of heaven is not, for the Jewish Jesus of Nazareth, a piece of real estate for a single saved soul; it is a communal vision of what could be and what should be.
—A.J. Levine, The Misunderstood Jew[3]

A father has brought his child to Jesus—to the disciples, actually—but the father insists he brought his child to Jesus, believing the disciples are the community of Jesus. And though the suffering of the child must have been shockingly apparent, the disciples do not focus on healing or even being present with the father and son; instead, the disciples stand around arguing theology with the scribes. It's a startling image. The father and son suffering on the margins, the disciples and scribes with their backs to this suffering caught up in a theological debate.

The story's details in a book known for its brevity are striking: the boy is inhabited by a spirit that robs him of speech and hearing, that causes him to go rigid and foam at the mouth, grind his teeth. The spirit seizes the child, throws him down, tosses him about, and pitches him into the fire and water, sucking the life out of him so that he appears to be dead.

But if the disciples turn away from the boy, Jesus brings the boy closer by giving his time and attention, by drawing him into the center of the story. Jesus asks the father how long this has been happening and then listens to the father's painfully detailed description of this terrorizing, life-destroying spirit. Jesus does not assume he knows what's happening, he asks and listens. When Jesus rebukes the spirit, things get worse instead of better so that those around him pronounce the child dead. But Jesus does not turn away, he does not give up, he does not "keep out of the way of knowing"[4] as the disciples seem to have done. Jesus stays, listens, engages the powers that are killing the boy, making sure that they will not return; he takes the boy by the hand, lifts him up, and returns him to community, whole, healed, and restored. Jesus embodies radical discipleship, and invites us to follow.

When we engaged Mark 9:14–29 through participatory Bible study inside a men's maximum security prison, those entering the story as the father confronted the scribes and the disciples. Repeatedly, they asked what it was that had prevented them from even turning to listen to the cries of the child or to their own pleas as the father. "For real," one of the men asked, "where's your head? Where's your heart? What got you all locked up so you can't even remember who you ought to be? I know you see us over here struggling."

But it was the group bringing voice to the boy that broke us open. As people from the group shared their own stories of terror and trauma, of being tossed about by poverty and racism, of being silenced and deafened by the labels placed on them at an early age, of being thrown in the fire by school systems so quick to tell them they would never measure up and might as well downsize their dreams now, of being beaten, neglected, and abused by folks who were meant to love them by definition, of being hungry and scared, homeless and cold, tortured and terrified. They turned to all of us—the scribes, the disciples, the crowd—and asked, "Where were the rest of you? We know you could see what was happening. We know you had to hear all the commotion this stuff caused, where were you?"

One of the participants who was in the group that was wrestling with how the child felt simply said, "This was me; me in school, hollering, disrupting, thrashing about. Angry, scared, mixed up. If somebody just would have been there for me, asked me what was happening, helped me through the madness, man, I could've been a contender."

And others added that it is when those whom we trust and whom we love don't hear our voices or when they are judgmental or do not see us, that is when you have to "allow your heart to be your ears." That is when you have to keep saying you deserve more and "you deserve better." One of the men grew quiet and in almost a whisper he said, "I've lived this story. I can't even say anything more cause this stuff is real for me."

And then the Jesus group responded. "I'm angry, torn, and at a loss for words," one said. "I am upset with the adults—these understudies who can't seem to do anything right. But I'm taken by the strength of this kid. Kid had heart. And he had a father who hung in there with him, doing all he could to make things better, trying to figure out how to set things right for his boy," another man added. "And I'm thankful he had someone," someone concluded. "How many don't have anyone paying attention or standing there with them?"

I know some of these men's stories well and for how many of them this is true. I remember some of their writings and am haunted by the ways that we have written them out of the story; am haunted by how we have labeled so many of God's children expendable, disposable. At a meeting with local church folks the day after this participatory study of Mark 9, we asked what it might mean for the church to move into communities of struggle—not with programs or projects, not with answers or solutions, but with questions and a willingness to listen long enough to really hear the impact of these death-dealing forces on children. How might it change our understanding of ministry, we asked, if we were persistently present in impoverished communities, especially communities of color, if we were identifying the already existing resources, leadership, and life-giving forces; if we were learning to identify and resist the systems and structures that rob children of their speech and hearing, that throw children around, that cause them to become rigid and lifeless, that seek to destroy the children from the day they are born? Systems that leave them out.

Marian Wright Edelman, founder and president of the Children's Defense Fund, the national child advocacy organization that coined the term "cradle-to-prison pipeline" writes

> *. . . incarceration is becoming the new American apartheid and poor children of color are the fodder. . . . Child poverty and neglect, racial disparities in systems that serve children and the pipeline to prison are not acts of God. They are America's immoral political and economic choices that can and must be changed with strong political, corporate and community leadership . . . We must all call for an investment in all children from birth through their successful transition to adulthood, remembering Frederick Douglass's correct observation that "it is easier to build strong children than to repair broken men."*[5]

The cradle-to-prison pipeline is the day-in-day-out systemic forces that target certain children from birth—especially children of color from impoverished communities. It is the name to the social and political forces that end up caging one out of every three black boys during their lives; that make it a likelihood that a third of black boys will one day end up in prison.[6] For those without a high school diploma, "that figure rises to about 60%."[7]

While these figures fluctuate depending on the state, and are hopefully decreasing as juvenile justice reforms make progress, they are a scandal. These numbers create an alarming backdrop to children. They emphasize the enormous impact that racism and poverty have on children. We criminalize children for status offenses, offenses that used to land students in detention, not jail. We criminalize roughhousing and what in other communities is laughed off as teenagers or young adults "sowing wild oats." Zero-tolerance school discipline policies have disproportionately impacted children of color; they have intensified racial disparities in this criminalization.[8]

"Black girls . . . face discriminatory school discipline at a starker level than even black boys. Black girls are six times as likely as white girls to be arrested on school grounds. While they represent only sixteen percent of the total female students, they make up thirty-four percent of the girls arrested on campus," notes an Institute for Policy Studies article on the matter.[9] Because of zero-tolerance school discipline policies, the number of police officers on school grounds have increased dramatically along with the number of school-based arrests. According to Monique Morris, author of *Pushout: The Criminalization of Black Girls in Schools*, black girls represent more than 50 percent of the girls who receive repeated out-of-school suspensions.[10] Morris notes that this targeting starts early. While black children represent 18 percent of the preschool enrollment, they represent 42 percent of preschool-aged children who are punished with out-of-school suspensions, most often charged with unruly or disruptive behavior.[11] A six-year-old black girl in Georgia was arrested and handcuffed for unruly behavior, as if adults could not imagine a different option for the child.[12]

Joseph, caged in a maximum security prison, joined one of the restorative justice college classes that takes place inside the prison in partnership with an inside leadership team. Half the students are from the outside and half are residents in the prison. In a letter Joseph wrote to congregations attending a speech by Michelle Alexander, author of *The New Jim Crow*, he says, " . . . these kids need people they can talk to. People who can help them identify the madness in their lives . . . Bring those kids in from the streets, hug them, and say to them, 'we love you,' and reinforce those words with your actions and commitment . . . At one point in my life I was these kids, I needed people like you in my life, but I did not know I could come to you, so I am coming to you for them."

Joseph wrote about his experience of sitting in class the night one of the co-facilitators asked everyone to answer the question, "What did you dream of growing up to be when you were young?" Joseph was startled because he suddenly realized he had never dreamed as a child. He writes,

> *I did not come from a loving, nurturing family. "MF, you little ugly MF." I could go on telling you how I was spoken to as a child but the words remain the same. . . . One day in class we were asked to tell people what you dreamed of being when you grew up. It got to me and I had to tell the class that I never had a dream of becoming anything in my life. My childhood was spent wanting my parents to love me, crying because I was hungry, or crying because one of them had hit me or hurt me with hollering. At the age of thirteen my mother tried to beat me to death. Those years were spent learning how to fight so I would never have to endure another beating like that by anyone. . . . I lived each day of life just surviving. . . . What if I would have known how to think and dream? What if I could have experienced the love that was so obvious in those young people's conversation? The love from family and friends that allowed them to dream. What if I had had a dream?*

According to a Sentencing Project's "Race and Punishment" report, whites in the United States associate people of color with criminality. And while two-thirds of African Americans see the criminal justice system as biased against blacks, only one-fourth of whites agree.[13] Nearly 60 percent of middle-aged African-American men without a high school degree have been caged in prison and one out of every nine prisoners is serving a life sentence. In Tennessee, that means someone given a life sentence, sixty years, will be caged for fifty-one years before there is any possibility of parole. As Harmon Wray, activist and proponent of restorative justice, writes, " . . . the criminal justice system is being used in our society as a force for racism, social control, patriarchy, and repression of dissent, and as a dumping ground for human beings regarded as toxic waste by the dominant sectors of our society."[14]

Romal Tune, author, spoken word artist, teacher, and poet, writes about his own experience with the systems that leave children out, that turn their backs on young folks. He writes,

> *By the time I was in the 8th grade I got tired of asking strangers if they had any change to spare and then watching them cross the street and look away like I wasn't even there. Even a blind man could see that society didn't care about people like me. I guess they figured it was my fault for being born in poverty . . . All I ever really wanted was a chance to be free, for society to stop judging me by their stereotypes and personal insecurities . . . How many kids are growing up just like me?*[15]

One of the alternative communities that makes sure children living in poverty, especially children of color, are seen, heard, cherished, affirmed, and empowered is the Children's Defense Fund's Freedom Schools. Rooted in the civil rights movement and the 1964 Mississippi Freedom Summer Project, Children's Defense Fund Freedom Schools invite children and their families and community to rename the world in defiance of all the systems and structures, institutions and theologies that label, limit, dismiss, diminish, exclude, and belittle them. Children's Defense Fund Freedom Schools encourage scholars—the children and youth—to see themselves as change agents, with abilities and gifts for repairing the world. Through Children's Defense Fund Freedom Schools, scholars recover cultural history, commit to reading and critical thinking, invest in conflict resolution and restorative justice practices, uncover their own good gifts, and learn to love themselves and to love learning. The very same students who were so quickly kicked out of public schools emerge as readers and writers, dancers and dreamers, artists and advocates, mentors and mediators, playwrights and poets. As Dr. John Hope Franklin, honorary chair of the Children's Defense Fund's Black Community Crusade for Children campaign, noted in 1995, "[We want to help our children develop] an understanding and appreciation for family, for their own rich heritage derived from their African forebears as well as their American experience, the kind of understanding that will simultaneously provide them with roots and wings."[16]

Their Freedom School teachers, servant-leader interns, are college students under the age of thirty who come from the same kinds of communities as the scholars and have survived similar struggles. These interns come together for training in nonviolent organizing and trauma-informed care, in literacy and culturally powerful resources, in conflict resolution and liberatory educational pedagogy. Working with the parents and others in the community, the servant-leader interns accompany the scholars in redefining education and creating a safe space where trauma and terror can be processed together and healing can begin. "Something inside so strong," we sing in Children's Defense Fund Freedom Schools, the words of a South African freedom song. The words assure us that we can make it in spite of all the barriers, because we know who we are and the gifts inside of us and our community. Standing among almost two thousand young servant-leader interns who are singing this song, dancing through the accompanying motions, pounding the floor with the rhythm of their feet, pouring their hearts into the words, is a glimpse into the kin-dom of God. This is the kin-dom that is experienced and understood, not as a piece of real estate for individuals, as Amy-Jill Levine, Jewish New Testament theologian and seminary professor, writes, but as one of communal salvation, collective liberation, a vision of God's shalom.

Patrick Reyes, Latinx scholar, organizer, and author, writes about the struggle for identity and culture, the struggle with the streets and schools, in his book *Nobody Cries When We Die: God, Community, and Surviving to Adulthood*. Reyes writes:

> You slay us in the classroom as quickly as we would have been slain on our streets. You enact a psychological violence on us that says we are not welcome, that we don't belong, that we are not to be breathing the same air as you . . . I understood in my bones that this struggle was about life . . . it was about the right to breathe, the right to live, the right to be a member of this human race . . . Survival is a communal act. When we hear the call to life, we must answer it. When we know that call is muted for others, we must find new ways to communicate it to them.[17]

"When we hear the call to life, we must answer it. When we know that call is muted for others, we must find new ways to communicate it to them." United Methodist Women has been steadfast in answering this call by partnering with Children's Defense Fund Freedom Schools across the nation, and by joining with others to celebrate the Children's Sabbath.

United Methodist Women is working to create safe spaces for children where they can not only survive, but also thrive. Partnering with Children's Defense Fund Freedom Schools, Children's Sabbath, and the Children's Defense Fund's annual Samuel DeWitt Proctor Institute for Child Advocacy and Ministry, United Methodist Women is working to become co-creators with God to make sure there are no children who are being left out and or made to feel like they do not belong, that they are not to breathe the same air. United Methodist Women answers this call to a radical discipleship and partnership again and again, knowing that survival is communal, that our lives and our kin-dom loving are bound together.

The Rev. Reginald Blount, United Methodist pastor and assistant professor of Faith, Youth, and Culture at Garrett-Evangelical Theological Seminary, worked with Virginia Lee and others at the seminary to create a Children's Defense Fund Freedom School. Blount explores what it might mean to move "From Sabbath Schools to Freedom Schools," what it might mean to redefine Christian education through the lens of the freedom movement, Blount writes that this

> *. . . is a call for the church to provide safe space for transformation and renewal to take place, using the language and culture of the "behind-the-wall" community and not that of the dominant culture . . . Freedom Schools are being conducted in 107 cities, and the majority of the sites are housed and run by local congregations. . . . If we believe that the purpose of Christian education is to set people free, then Christian education must continue to commit itself to being that catalyst in removing barriers that keep persons from fulfilling their call to serve as God's agent, steward, and partner in the caring and re-creating of God's creation."*[18]

In the core syllabus created by theological educators for seminarians enrolled in the Children's Defense Fund's Proctor Institute for Child Advocacy's seminary course, the learning goal is "to reframe and transform religious leadership in view of the sacrality and integrity of every child, every youth." All children, all youth, are sacred. As Jesus says at the end of Mark 9, the greatest is "whoever welcomes" a child. Whoever takes the child in their arms, holds them safe, and affirms their value and dignity, "whoever welcomes one such child in my name welcomes me," Jesus tell us. And he expands this: "whoever welcomes me welcomes . . . the one who sent me" (Mark 9:37). In the following chapter, Jesus again says, "Let the little children come to me" (Mark 10:13–15). God's kin-dom belongs to the most vulnerable, the children. If we are not in solidarity with the most vulnerable; if we are not including, affirming, and loving little ones, we cannot, Jesus says, enter the reign of God.

John Wesley knew this and argued that Methodist preachers were required to spend time with children, whether they had gifts for this work or not. No negotiation, no assigning this task of proximity to the children's ministry task force—children are a priority for Jesus and therefore must be a priority for Methodist preachers. Wesley pushed Methodists to spend time with those who are impoverished, with children who are hungry and hurting, with those battered by the dominant systems and theologies. He insisted that unless we immerse ourselves among the vulnerable, impoverished, imprisoned, we cannot hear the gospel and cannot be the church of Jesus Christ. He writes:

> *One reason why the rich in general have so little sympathy for the poor is because they so seldom visit them. Hence it is that, according to the common observation, one part of the world does not know what the other suffers. Many of them do not know because they do not care to know; they keep out of the way of knowing it—and then plead their voluntary ignorance as an excuse for their hardness of heart.*[19]

Do we "keep out of the way of knowing?" And, how is it that so many of our churches have limited children's and youth ministries to just the children of church members, rather than ministry with the millions of children who are hungry for identity and belonging, who ache for a place to belong and a safe space for healing? What would it look like if churches began to redefine children's and youth ministry in response to the crisis created by the cradle-to-prison pipeline, racism, and poverty? What would it look like to put the child at the center of the story and, as a church, not turn our backs? In Nicaragua, after the Sandinistas came to power, a children's park was built with a sign saying, "and only the children will be privileged." What does Mark invite us to take up today so that we can be present with those littlest, most vulnerable ones? What, in a practice of radical discipleship, might need to change in our lives, churches, communities, nations, and world if children are to be the ones privileged by our policies and priorities, budgets and buildings, systems and structures, institutions and theologies? What liberation and life might be ushered in when we see all children as our children—as children of God.

The disciples and scribes seem deaf to the cries of the father and blind to the ongoing struggles of the child. They are busy arguing theology. What distances us from the hurt and hope of children and youth caught in poverty, racism, and other systems of violence? How might we create and support communities where healing happens and hope is reborn, even while we are working to dismantle the structures and systems that perpetuate the oppression?

Marian Wright Edelman demands that we do better. She declares,

> *It is unconscionable that our rich nation lets one fifth of our children live in poverty. It is intolerable that our nation with the most advanced medical technology allows millions of children to lack health care and the opportunity to see a doctor when they are sick or to get preventative care. It is unacceptable that millions of children are waiting for a quality Head Start or child care program to get ready for school. It is profoundly immoral that we let the lottery of geography or race or class determine a child's chances in life and act as if God created children as haves or have-nots.*[20]

Jonathan Kozol, writer, educator, and activist, has been exposing this immorality and challenging these life-diminishing forces for more than fifty years. He does so by being among, listening to, learning from, and being challenged by those living in impoverished communities, especially the children. In the introduction to *Amazing Grace*, Kozol writes,

> *. . . when I look for hope these days, I tend to look less often to external signs of progress such as housing reconstruction—which can be too rapidly arrested and reversed by shifts in public policy—than to the words and prayers of children and the spiritual resilience of so many of their mothers and grandmothers. It is, above all, the very young whose luminous capacity for tenderness and love and a transcendent sense of faith in human decency give me reason for hope.*[21]

Kozol's landmark book might serve as a map for a congregation's ministry with and among impoverished children. Kozol describes a small neighborhood church as a "gentle sanctuary from the terrors of the streets outside."[22] One pastor in the book comments, "We see God as a liberating force who calls us to deliver people from oppression."[23]

Personal Reflection:
Wrestling with Radical Discipleship

The Rev. Bill Barnes, my pastor, beloved friend, prophet, and mentor, was a United Methodist pastor who started the first intentionally multiracial congregation in Nashville. He also spent more than thirty years nurturing this congregation located in the garage of a house in one of the most impoverished neighborhoods in the city. Bill was a theologian and organizer, author and agitator, who embodied kin-dom living and loving. He was a relentless freedom fighter—from the beginnings of the civil rights movement until the day he died—insisting on embodied justice and life-giving liberation. He played the guitar and sang joyfully and heartily, often making up songs. One day after he had retired, he was out walking in the neighborhood and a boy of about eight ran up to him and asked, "Hey, aren't you the COG man?" "Why yes, I am," Bill responded, "and so are you!" And then they sang together one of Bill's songs, "You are a COG! A what? A child of God! You are a WOG! A what? A wonder of God! You are a GOG! A what? A gift of God!" And on and on it went as they danced down the street.

How did you come to believe that being a child of God, a gift of God, is the deepest truth about who you are? How might you and your congregation be involved in partnering with families and children in impoverished communities, especially children of color, so that they come to know, deep down inside, that they are COGs, WOGs, GOGs? Find out if there are any Children's Defense Fund Freedom Schools in your community and, if not, explore what it might take to get one started. What might a community-wide Children's Sabbath look like? Or a Child Watch Team that goes to find out more about your juvenile court and detention center?

Explore the possibility of sending a team of people from your congregation, perhaps teams from several congregations, to actively

continued on page 86

continued from page 85

participate in and gain skills through the Children's Defense Fund's Samuel DeWitt Proctor Institute for Child Advocacy, which takes place the third week of every July. Work with the Children's Defense Fund, with United Methodist Women, and others to dismantle the cradle-to-prison pipeline, especially as it impacts children of color. What might it mean to redefine Christian education and children's and youth ministries through the lens of the sacrality of every child? Find out more by visiting the Children's Defense Fund and United Methodist Women websites: **childrensdefense.org** and **unitedmethodistwomen.org/racialjustice/school2prisonpdf.**

NOTES

ENDNOTES

1. Oscar Romero, *The Violence of Love: The Pastoral Wisdom of Archbishop Oscar Romero*, compiled and translated by James Brockman (San Francisco: Harper & Row, Publishers, 1988), 242.

2. C.S. Song, *Jesus and the Reign of God* (Minneapolis: Fortress Press, 1993), 147.

3. Amy-Jill Levine, *The Misunderstood Jew: The Church and the Scandal of the Jewish Jesus* (San Francisco: HarperOne, 2007), 51.

4. Pamela Couture, *Seeing Children, Seeing God: A Practical Theology of Children and Poverty* (Nashville: Abingdon Press, 2000), 56.

5. See "The Cradle to Prison Pipeline Campaign: America's New Apartheid," Children's Defense Fund, accessed September 11, 2017, childrensdefense.org/child-watch-columns/health/2009/the-cradle-to-prison-pipeline-americas-new-apartheid.

6. "Cradle to Prison Pipeline Campaign," Children's Defense Fund.

7. Michelle Alexander, "Women of Spirit" (lecture, Union Theological Seminary, New York, March 4, 2015), 2.

8. See Bryan Stevenson, *Just Mercy: A Story of Justice and Redemption* (New York: Spiegel & Grau, 2014), 155. "In poor urban neighborhoods across the United States, black and brown boys routinely have multiple encounters with the police. Even though many of these children have done nothing wrong, they are targeted by police, presumed guilty, and suspected by law enforcement of being dangerous or engaged in criminal activity. The random stops, questioning, and harassment dramatically increase the risk of arrest for petty crimes. Many of these children develop criminal records for behavior that more affluent children engage in with impunity."

9. Katie Jones, "American Schools Are Criminalizing Black Girls," Institute for Policy Studies, April 22, 2016, ips-dc.org/american-schools-criminalizing-black-girls.

10. Monique W. Morris, Pushout: *The Criminalization of Black Girls in School* (New York: The New Press, 2016), 68.

11. Ibid., 57.

ENDNOTES *continued*

12. Ibid., 4.

13. Available at "Race and Punishment: Racial Perceptions of Crime and Support for Punitive Policies," The Sentencing Project, 2014, sentencingproject.org/wp-content/uploads/2015/11/Race-and-Punishment.pdf.

14. Harmon Wray and Laura Magnioni, *Beyond Prisons: A New Interfaith Paradigm for Our Failed Prison System* (Minneapolis: Fortress Press, 2006), 88.

15. Romal Tune, "Who's Looking for Me?" YouTube video, 4:07 minutes, June 3, 2014, youtube.com/watch?v=5e7yzIrjpbI.

16. "CDF Freedom Schools Program," Children's Defense Fund, accessed September 8, 2017, childrensdefense.org/programs/freedomschools.

17. Patrick Reyes, *Nobody Cries When We Die: God, Community, and Surviving to Adulthood* (Saint Louis, MO: Chalice Press, 2016), 163.

18. Reginald Blount, "From Sabbath Schools to Freedom Schools," in *Educating for Redemptive Community: Essays in Honor of Jack Seymour and Margaret Ann Cain*, ed. Denise Janssen (Eugene, OR: Wipf & Stock, 2015), 71, 76.

19. Couture, 56.

20. Marian Wright Edelman, draft chapter to be included in a book on Howard Thurman, edited by Greg Ellison, forthcoming.

21. Jonathan Kozol, *Amazing Grace: The Lives of Children and the Conscience of a Nation* (New York: Crown Publishers, 1995), xiv–xv.

22. Ibid., 6.

23. Ibid., 80–81.

Chapter 4

Sabbath Economics: Mark 10:17–31

A church that does not join the poor in order to speak out from the side of the poor against the injustices committed against them is not the true church of Jesus Christ.
—Oscar Romero, February 17, 1980[1]

It is a caricature of love to try to cover over with alms what is lacking in justice, to patch over with an appearance of benevolence when social justice is missing.
—Oscar Romero, April 12, 1979[2]

Jesus, looking at him, loved him and said, "You lack one thing; go, sell what you own, and give the money to the poor, and you will have treasure in heaven; then come, follow me. . . . How hard it will be for those who have wealth to enter the kingdom of God!"
—Mark 10:21, 23

What does it mean to be loved by Jesus? Mark 10:21 is the only time in the Synoptic Gospel texts that a writer says Jesus loved someone and it is the same Greek word used in the verse, "For God so loved the world . . ." (John 3:16). This is not the Hallmark card version of love, not a soft sentimentality oozing comfort without cost. It is a fierce love that liberates and makes new. This is a love that means to free us from all that keeps us in bondage, from all that prevents us from being who God created us to be, from all that limits kin-dom living. And, as Mark notes, it is not always heard as good news.

Jesus' love was not received as good news by the man who had run up to Jesus, knelt before him, and asked what must be done to inherit eternal life. Jesus' response seems abrupt, rude even. Jesus challenges the man for calling him "good," and then declares that the man already knows what to do, the commandments have outlined it clearly. But the man persists, arguing that he has already shaped his life through the keeping of these commandments. And then Jesus, loving this man, issues the invitation "sell what you own, and give the money to the poor . . . then come, follow me" (Mark 10:21). The text is clear on how this good news was received: the man—shocked—"went away grieving, for he had many possessions" (Mark 10:22).

Ched Myers, who coined the term "Sabbath economics," notes, "Jesus dismisses the worldview that equates wealth and power with divine blessing or human meritocracy."[3] And to make sure no one misses the clear challenge to the exploitative economic systems that produce wealth, Jesus rewords one of the commandments from "do not covet" to "do not defraud," emphasizing what Myers terms the "cycle of indebtedness . . . [and how wealth is] the result of illegitimate expropriation of their neighbor's land . . . Jesus is not inviting this man to change his attitude toward his wealth, nor to treat his servants better, nor to reform his personal life. He is asserting the precondition for discipleship: economic justice."[4] Jesus binds together our salvation and our possessions—our faith and our economic entanglements—and does all of this through the language of love.

The disciples struggle to comprehend Jesus' words—they are "perplexed" and "greatly astounded," feeling so stunned by this hard challenge that they wonder if it's possible for anyone to be saved. Twice Jesus notes how hard it is for those who have wealth to enter the kin-dom of God. Many of the disciples left families and homes, possessions and property in order to become partners in this beloved community and yet they struggle to understand what Jesus means in this story.

The difference between the disciples and the rich man is that the disciples in this story do not walk away. They may be confused and even sorrowful, but they stay to wrestle with these hard words from Jesus. What is it about wealth that prevents us from participating in the kin-dom of God? How do we hear this text if we are among the economically secure and powerful? How do we learn to pray "Thy kingdom come" in a world that so clearly clashes with the kin-dom of God? How do we let go of our possessions, of all that possesses us? Alan Storey, Methodist pastor in South Africa, notes, "It is easier to believe in the resurrected body of the dead than to believe in radical economic transformation."[5]

This is a powerful claim and one that is not only born out of an assessment from the pulpit, but also in research conducted around these questions of Christianity and economics. A 2017 survey of 1,686 Americans by *The Washington Post* and the Kaiser Family Foundation asked if the survey participants believed people were poor because of some individual failing on their part or because of something beyond their control. Forty-six percent of those identifying themselves as Christians responded that poverty was more often the fault of the individual, while only twenty-nine percent of those identifying as non-Christians believed it was due to individual failings.[6]

According to the analysis of *The Washington Post* survey, those identifying themselves as white evangelical Protestants were 3.2 times as likely to blame poverty on the poor rather than on systems and structures that perpetuate poverty. While responders noted that their congregations were not uncaring about the poor and in fact invested often a great deal in a variety of charitable efforts, many theologians drew a sharp distinction between charity and justice. The Rev. Dr. Jacqui Lewis, senior minister at Middle Collegiate Church in New York City, argues there is a deep theological and moral problem with offering charity to the poor while at the same time blaming them for their poverty. Responding to the poll, Lewis commented:

> *We are forced to ask ourselves about whether the ways these systems work are consistent and coherent with our belief in a God of love and justice, whose compassion was shown uniquely in the life of a poor Jewish Rabbi from Palestine . . . We have to ask ourselves are we following in the Way of Christ or are we following in the Way of Empire.*[7]

This is a Jesus question—one he repeats often. From the beginning, the good news of God has been a direct confrontation with the powers that be, with the status quo. Jesus, born among an impoverished people, survivor of an economy that left most human beings on the edges, creator of a community in which possessions were few and wealth was equitably redistributed, teacher who declared the first would be last and the last would be first, theologian who framed everything through the lens of those who were impoverished and oppressed, healer and liberator who repeatedly challenged the death-dealing structures and theologies that propped up poverty and other forms of violence; *Jesus* exposes our seduction by and complicity with empire.

Peter Storey, former Methodist bishop of Southern Africa, argues that our complicity with domination is the result of our proximity to Caesar, the wealthy, and our distance from the poor. He writes,

> *The public square has been captured . . . by those who offer a religious face to power, to economic greed, to its accompanying violence . . . John Wesley's transformation into an evangelist who evangelized not just individuals, but the institutions in society, was all about location . . . When John Wesley was with the poor, he found that he had unknowingly arrived at the home address of Jesus . . . Why is it that the United Methodist Church seems to have lost its prophetic voice? . . . Because it's rich . . . It has become a church of the comfortable. It has become the church of the middle class and the affluent . . . The Methodist Church in Southern Africa was able to make the stand that it did because 80% of our members were from the poor and oppressed.*[8]

John Wesley understood that Sabbath economics are not held up by individuals, but collectively—by communities. The importance of proximity was precisely what John Wesley argued, fearing that Methodists would become a church of the affluent. As Theodore Jennings notes in his book, *Good News to the Poor: John Wesley's Evangelical Economics*, Wesley was convinced that a church that did not weigh everything through a social location among and with the poor could not be the church of Jesus Christ. In fact, Wesley's words are far harsher than those of Jesus. Wesley had no doubt that wealth prevents us from participating in the realm, the kin-dom of God. Wesley notes, "By riches I mean, not thousands of pounds, but any more than will procure the conveniences of life. Thus I account him a rich man who has food and raiment for himself and his family, without running into debt . . . the accumulation of property must be viewed concretely as theft!"[9]

Wesley considered money squandered on fancy clothes to be a sin. "Surely," he tells us, "you cannot be ignorant, that the sinfulness of fine apparel lies chiefly in the expensiveness. In that it is robbing God and the poor; it is defrauding the fatherless and widow; it is wasting that food of the hungry, and withholding his raiment from the naked to consume it on our own lusts."[10]

Wesley cautions against building big buildings and fancy churches, arguing that if we build anything more than is plain and absolutely necessary, we will then be dependent upon the wealthy, and lose the gospel as a result. Challenging contemporary notions of stewardship, Wesley argues that stewardship means redistributing resources among and with those who are impoverished. As Jennings writes, summing up Wesley's notes on stewardship, "We give to God not by giving to the church, but by giving to the poor . . . it is the practice of solidarity with the poor."[11]

Bill Wylie-Kellermann, United Methodist pastor and theologian, author and activist living in Detroit, notes that Wesley focuses on the violence of the economic systems and seeks to create a Methodist movement that confronts not simply individual moral failings, but also the deadly structures of empire and global economic violence. It is not enough for us as individuals to avoid personal sins, we must also be aware of our complicity with the systems that perpetuate injustices and oppression—our collective sinning. Wesley argues that it is our captivity in and cooperation with the economic system that stands in the way of discipleship. He writes:

> *Now, it is your money that pays the merchant, and through him the captain and the African butchers. You therefore are guilty, yeah, principally guilty, of all these frauds, robberies, and murders. You are the spring that puts all the rest in motion; they would not stir a step without you; therefore the blood of all these wretches who die before their time, whether in their country or elsewhere, lies upon your head . . . Instantly, at any price, were it the half of your goods, deliver thyself from blood-guiltiness! Thy hands, thy bed, thy furniture, thy house, thy lands, are at present stained with blood.*[12]

Toward the end of his life, a time when the Methodist movement was thriving in terms of numbers, membership, and church growth, Wesley cautions:

> *I am not afraid that the people called Methodist should ever cease to exist . . . But I am afraid, lest they should only exist as a dead sect, having the form of religion without the power . . . It nearly concerns us to understand how the case stands with us at present. I fear, wherever riches have increased . . . the essence of religion, the mind that was in Christ, has decreased in the same proportion.*[13]

In his foreword to the Kinslers' book, *The Biblical Jubilee and the Struggle for Life*, Ched Myers extends this critique. Quoting the American Jesuit theologian John Haughey who laments, "We read the gospel as if we had no money . . . and we spend our money as if we know nothing of the gospel," Myers addresses the centrality of the economy to the gospel. Myers writes:

> *Indeed, the topic of economics is exceedingly difficult to introduce in most First World churches—more taboo than politics or even sex. Yet no aspect of our individual and corporate lives is more determinative of our welfare, and few subjects are more frequently addressed in our Scriptures. The standard of economic and social justice is woven into the warp and woof of the Bible. Pull this strand and the whole fabric unravels.*[14]

One of the churches I worked with in Nashville might have identified with this wealthy man whom Jesus loved, this powerful man who walks away grieving. Birthed by their participation in the southern Methodist split over slavery, this congregation built its first sanctuary in 1851. They received Civil War reparation funds after the Union Army occupied their sanctuary, and with those funds, the congregation bought land nearby, building a sanctuary there in 1867. This building later became a Christian education wing as the congregation's growth spilled over into a new sanctuary in 1929, and a new parsonage and an additional building for offices and a library were built in 1952. In the 1950s, the congregation had more than 1,500 members, mostly from the surrounding wealthy white neighborhood. Powerful politicians knew they needed to come by this congregation in order to be elected. The choir was known across the country, the organ was famous, and a large number of recognized civic leaders were members.

But as urban neighborhood populations shifted, and many wealthy, white families moved to the suburbs, membership declined. By the early 1990s, the congregation had an average of thirty people in Sunday worship, most over the age of sixty-five and little, if any, ongoing connection with the new neighbors living nearby. Struggling to pay utility bills and keep up with maintenance on the huge buildings, the congregation grew anxious. They considered renting out the parsonage, selling off a part of the land that was still open unoccupied space, or perhaps moving renters into the Christian education building. But it is hard to let go of possessions, of all that possesses us. When we become anxious, afraid of the future, we most often cling even more tightly to the familiar.

Good news, though—what looked impossible to Jesus' disciples is possible through God's power, and this stage of our isolated and anxious church was not the end of the story. However, our transformation was not easy or quick, and there were some leaders who walked away, sorrowful and grieving. But for those who stayed, the transformation began with participatory Bible study, similar to the stories I have included here in this book. It was not long before the congregation noted that the Bible often pulls us where we do not want to go, inviting us to let go when we would much rather hold on, startling us with radical discipleship and shaking us up with the images of what it might mean to be the church of Jesus Christ in and for and with the world around us. It was clear though, early on, that no matter how hard we tried, we would not find biblical images of church or discipleship that would settle for simply showing up on Sundays for worship.

While it took eleven different votes to find consensus and clarity, the congregation did decide to transfer the vacant land to Habitat for Humanity. Our partnership with Habitat to build five single-family homes and a community playground, though, was not without controversy. Our decision that came out of a wrestling with Jesus' message was not quite met with persecution, but it was met with a lot of difficulty: meetings with the surrounding community, repeated reminders that no, we could not choose the families who would move into the houses, and no, we could not require them to be Christians or attend church. But the transformation was stunning. Our tightly clenched hands and hearts, minds and spirits, buildings and boundaries, began to open and we stumbled together into new life.

In a matter of ten days, working with more than thirty congregations and organizations and more than five hundred volunteers, the Habitat houses were completed. This was a miracle of biblical proportions that everyone recognized. It was a miracle in that it changed our identity. We were no longer a dying congregation, but a community through which God was doing something new. It was a miracle because it changed our hearts, our minds, our practices, and patterns of being church. And it called us to repentance and we asked together: if God can do this much with the little bit we weren't even using, imagine what might result from letting go of more?

It was neighborhood children walking in to our worship services who turned us upside down and right-side up. They came alone, without parents, and most came with no church experience. Where adults saw decaying buildings needing massive amounts of money, the children saw great halls with space for their pictures on the walls, pictures that would still be there days later. They found a kitchen that still had a working refrigerator, discovered a stage for their creativity, and made themselves at home in a safe space where they did not have to look over their shoulders. The congregation had prayed for children to come, but I'm not sure they were expecting these particular children—children who came laughing and loud, disrupting and disturbing, demanding attention and time and space. At one point, the congregation decided we should create a children's ministry committee in order to deal with the uproar, and so they announced their intention and a meeting time during worship. When we entered the room for the meeting, it was already filled with children who exclaimed, "We didn't know adults came to children's meetings!" We were transformed by the children who taught us to let go, over and over again. To let go of the rule that said no refreshments in the parlor. To let go of the notion that bulletins could contain worship. To let go of silence and predictability—of doing things the way we were used to doing them. They exposed so many of our settled assumptions.

Somewhere in the process of becoming a church, we had initiated a time of sharing prayer concerns and celebrations during worship even though most of the congregation remained silent during this time. Children excelled in their participation. They could go on and on: "Spaghetti!" "Wow, this dog I saw that was really dirty and scary and then he licked my hand and didn't even bite!" "My mama came back."

One week, our church decided to include index cards in the bulletin and asked everyone to fill one out and turn it in during the offering time. If you couldn't write, you could draw a picture. At the end of the service we would each take a card home to pray over someone else's struggles and celebrations. Early on, we debated whether children should be allowed to take a prayer card home. "What if they couldn't read," some asked, or "what if they didn't really understand what was on the card—what if they didn't take it seriously?" And then one day, we discovered several of the children with worn and tattered prayer cards in their pockets. Having refused to throw them away, they continued to carry the cards wherever they went.

One Sunday, a seven-year-old girl tried to get my attention, waving her prayer card. But it wasn't time for prayer and so I nodded to her but did not invite her to speak. This happened several times and then finally she simply stood up, held up her prayer card, and shouted out, "I want you to pray for my friend who got killed and for all the kids who aren't dead yet." She had been standing next to a boy who was shot in crossfire in her low-income housing project and she had drawn a picture of herself standing next to his bleeding body. The moment changed everyone present.

The children came with so much heart and joy. In spite of the poverty, in spite of the systemic and daily racism and violence they walked through every day, in spite of the schools that were so quick to push them out, in spite of the adults who were all too often sources of hurt instead of help, they came dancing and dreaming, laughing and loving, singing and hoping, delighting in little things, finding so many reasons for rejoicing. And along the way, teaching us to be the church.

It was people from the streets who broke us open and brought new life. I remember one Sunday morning when I invited people to offer prayer concerns and celebrations, Roger stood up—he was living on the streets, struggling with mental illness, and had been coming to church for several weeks. He often offered celebrations and concerns, sometimes going on a little too long, and I had meant to talk with him about keeping his offerings just a bit shorter. But I had forgotten and now Roger was standing up, starting in on his request.

"I want a job," he told us. "I want a job so I can go in a store and pick out whatever shirt I want and buy it and take it home. I don't want to beg; I want a job so I can buy a shirt. I want a job so I can take my new shirt to the laundromat and wash it and wear it again. I want . . . "

And then he took a breath. And as soon as he did I interrupted and said, "Thank you, Roger. We're going to pray that you get a job." He had started to sit down but as soon as he heard my words he stood back up and shouted, "I don't want your damn prayers; I want a job."

After I got over the shock of hearing a swear word uttered in our worship service, I realized Roger spoke truth. Every Sunday there was someone in the congregation who had the capacity to offer Roger, and others, jobs. And I wondered how often we had been putting things on our prayer lists, our lists of things we hoped God would do, instead of using the resources already among us to address the needs. The Sabbath economics that had led us to open the doors of our church kept opening more and more. We began to see together the resources we all had and could share. And we saw how much more some of us understood about poverty and about having backs up against the wall than others; how much the rest of us could learn.

The people facing hard times, though, knew much more than just hardships. People from the streets, people with their backs up against the wall, knew so much and taught the rest of us so much about joy. While I had been a part of congregations that were verbally responsive, participatory congregations in which it is common for worshipers to comment aloud, this congregation before the Habitat experience had been decidedly silent. But folks from the streets could not hide their joy at encountering gospel good news that clearly exposed the lies of the world's consistently bad news for them, gospel good news that insisted they were cherished by God here and now just as they were. "Ain't God good!" folks would shout, "You know I'm right," the refrain.

When someone who was houseless became a member of the trustee committee, we began reimagining what we might do with the buildings and space. And when someone living on the streets became a member of the finance committee, we stopped postponing ministry until we had enough money. We were challenged again and again by a Sabbath economics to recognize the riches among us and redistribute money and power, decision-making and authority, resources and privilege.

Jim Lawson, United Methodist pastor, professor, and the man Dr. Martin Luther King Jr. referred to as "the leading non-violent strategist and theorist in the world," writes:

> *Moses' life is abruptly, and without explanation, changed. After his encounter with God, he is essentially radically and eternally changed. His transformation causes him to hear and see and observe and feel and grieve. So Moses alters his life and confounds his own people and the Pharaoh, who stood as a symbol of the systems of inequities. Similarly, Jesus, in the spirit, walks into the temple in Nazareth and declares fulfilled the prophecies of Isaiah to rewind the traditional and historic message of salvation. Christianity largely seems to ignore these two major, saving enterprises of the Bible . . . Americans codified the spiritual wickedness of racism, violence, impoverishment and greed . . . we human beings will often develop a theology which justifies our inexcusable behavior.*[15]

It is still startling to me that we are so good at these justifications that we can even fool ourselves into not hearing Jesus' words. We, who have more than we need, struggle so hard with the gospel's good news. We bend it all kinds of ways, trying to make it fit in to our lives and the world around us. Meanwhile, people surviving on the streets immediately hear the radicality, immediately see the truth of Jesus' call to radical discipleship in Mark. Many texts are hard for congregations with any amount of wealth to hear. Not only this text in Mark, but Matthew's text noting that the prostitutes and tax collectors will enter into the kin-dom of God before the religious authorities and theologians, before the bishops and high steeple clergy (Matthew 21:31). Or Jesus' clear declaration in Luke: "Blessed are you who are poor for yours is the kingdom of God . . . But woe to you who are rich . . . " (Luke 6:20, 24).

Consider how often we miss the sharp edges of the gospel because we are not among and not with those who are impoverished and violated. Mark 12:41–44 offers the story about the widow's offering, a story often used as a stewardship sermon exhorting us to give all we can—to the church.

But, if we listen to what comes before and after this story, the context provides the clue. Jesus marches into Jerusalem and straight into the temple, looks around, and then leaves (Mark 11:11). He returns to the temple to drive out sellers and buyers. He overturns the tables; he is visibly angry, not only confronting but dismantling the temple's marketplace economics (11:15–16). Later he returns again, walks into the temple and argues with the chief priests, scribes, and elders (11:27–33). And then, just before the story of the widow's mite, Jesus is seen teaching in the temple, harshly denouncing the scribes, saying, "They devour widows' houses" (12:40a).

Then, Jesus sits down opposite the temple and he watches as people put their money into the treasury. He comments about the poor widow who puts in "all she had to live on" (12:44). And Jesus at once walks away from the temple, countering the disciples' praise of the grand buildings and elegant stones, with the harsh declaration of destruction—"Not one stone will be left" (13:1–2).

And yet, it was not until I was in a battered women's shelter that I first heard the radical truth of this story. The women, eagerly engaged in a participatory Bible study with the text, noted that Jesus is not praising the woman, he's hollering at the folks who are ripping her off. He's unmasking the pious prayers for what they are: cover-ups for sucking the life out of the poor, taking the last little bit they've got left.

Or consider the story in Mark 14:3–9 in which the unnamed woman barges into the male gathering and anoints Jesus, pouring the contents of her alabaster jar over Jesus' head. The male disciples immediately condemn the woman, arguing that she should have sold the ointment and given the money to the poor. Then and now, disciples have focused not on Jesus' celebration of this woman's fierce faith and creative courage, but on taking the prior comments of Jesus out of context in order to smooth out the sharp edges and inevitable conflict. Jesus' words, "you will always have the poor with you," have been domesticated and most often used to justify the inevitability of poverty in defiance of this Jesus who argues for a Sabbath economics; who argues that economic justice is a condition for discipleship.

Jesus does not say there will always be people condemned to poverty; he says the poor will always be with and among us. The Jesus movement, the communities of Jesus' followers, takes sides with the poor. Like Jesus and John Wesley, they locate themselves among the impoverished, working not simply for charity but for justice. They work for an economic system in which there are no wealth disparities, in which the policies and practices of Sabbath economics redistribute wealth and resources, power and privilege, so that everyone has enough. As Ched Myers notes, "In capitalism, redistributive justice is high heresy—but this Jesus has clearly equated it with the Kingdom of God . . . economics is ultimately a theological issue."[16]

Sabbath economies shift the work of the church from charity to justice, recognizing that charity is its own form of violence. It robs people of their identity and vocation. Instead of their God-given identity as a child of God, they become objects of our charity. Instead of their God-given vocation of partnering with God to repair the world, their vocation becomes offering gratitude to those of us who give from our surplus. Charity lets us feel good even while we are propping up the very systems that make folks poor in the first place.

How is it that we so easily turn Jesus' often harsh, always challenging invitation to right-relationship, radical discipleship, troubling transformation into a comforting, soothing message with no sharp edges? How is it that we so easily domesticate the hard demand to untangle ourselves from systems and structures of oppression into something like writing a check? I am reminded of our congregation that had grown from a small handful of white-haired and white-knuckled churchgoers to a full and loud and out loud–loving church.

Lee Camp, in his book *Mere Discipleship* notes:

> *I write with a sense of burden, suspecting that even the religious rhetoric that appears to take Jesus seriously has domesticated him, cleaned him up, made him respectable so as not to embarrass us good church-going folk with our agendas of upward social mobility and social "responsibility," and in so doing has limited the answers believed to be possible or sensible or respectable to that commonly asked question, "What would Jesus do?"*[17]

Camp is right. Our answers get domesticated and shrink. And not only do our answers get smaller, but part of what a Sabbath economics offers is a recognition that our answers won't even be close to good news unless the partnerships are real and ongoing. We have to keep being reminded, we have to keep listening, we have to keep being on the side of the poor. That's how we can see what the good news really is.

Jesus invites the wealthy man and the disciples—all of us who seek to follow Jesus—to disengage from economic systems in which a few profit at the expense of the many, in which wealth comes directly from and through the systems and theologies of exploitation. Jesus pulls us out of Caesar's economies and into God's economy of manna and mercy. It is an economy learned in the wilderness school with the freedom-seeking Moses and Miriam, an economy in which there is enough for everyone and so everyone gathers only what we need for the moment. If someone hoards the manna, it rots, as a reminder that there really is enough if we share and take only what we need.

The economy of manna and mercy is a Sabbath economy; it is an economy of grace in contrast to all the economies of greed, and it marks the people of God as a covenant people. The seventh day, the Sabbath, is a reminder of who we are to be as the people of God, and how God intends for us to live in stark contrast to the world around us. Every Sabbath confronts and exposes our complicity with Pharaoh's economy and our silence in a world of economic violence. Structural economic violence is the most pervasive form of violence in the Bible and in our world, although in our world it is often the hardest violence for those of privilege to see. Dr. Martin Luther King Jr. spoke prophetically about this systemic violence and held it up to the light as he stood with sanitation workers in Memphis, wrote sermons calling out economic injustices and calling us in to right living, and asked—resoundingly, powerfully—what it serves a man to be able to sit at the counter if he can't afford to buy the food. King draws together the violence of racism, economic exploitation, militarism, and empire and calls for a sharp and righteous maladjustment to these systems telling us:

> *There are some things in our social system to which all of us ought to be maladjusted . . . I never intend to adjust myself to the evil of segregation and the crippling effects of discrimination. I never intend to adjust myself to the inequalities of an economic system which takes necessities from the masses to give luxuries to the classes. I never intend to become adjusted to the madness of militarism and the self-defeating methods of physical violence . . . It may be that the salvation of the world lies in the hands of the maladjusted.*[18]

But this call is not a call that ends in misery. It is not a call that has to end in sorrow, like the man hearing Jesus' news. Every Sabbath confronts and exposes our complicity with Pharaoh's economy. But, it is an invitation into salvation, into community, into the joy of seeing the world as it is; the Sabbath and Sabbath economics are an invitation to hear the good news of the Bible and the good news of Jesus. It leads us, like in our once-small and frail congregation, to move joyfully, loudly once again towards the Jesus question: where is life? And to follow that question to where it might take us.

The wilderness school of manna and mercy creates systems to remind us that we are to be an alternative community of Sabbath economics, nonviolent economics. That's why every seventh day and every seventh year the covenant God requires a reckoning with patterns and practices, policies and procedures, systems and structures to expose how we have become complicit with Egypt's economy of violence. And the requirements are very concrete: forgive debts, free debtors and indentured servants, restore and redistribute lands, remembering who and whose you are. And then every fiftieth year is Jubilee, a redistribution of wealth and reinvestment in structures and systems, patterns and practices that embody Sabbath economics. Imagine what that might look like in South Africa or Nicaragua or the United States—first, an exposure of the economic consequences of centuries of empire economics and then a redefinition of the economy that would have both reparations to address prior thefts and laws and policies to assure future equitable distribution of land and resources.[19]

Jesus is steeped in the traditions and scriptures of the prophets. He thunders like Isaiah, "It is you who have devoured the vineyard; the spoil of the poor is in your houses. What do you mean by crushing my people, by grinding the face of the poor? says the Lord God of hosts" (Isaiah 3:14b–15). Jesus declares with Ezekiel, "The people of the land have practiced extortion and committed robbery; they have oppressed the poor and needy, and have extorted from the alien without redress" (Ezekiel 22:29). Jesus echoes Micah's reminder that we must do justice and love mercy, reminding us that God is not satisfied with individual piety (Micah 6:8). As the Episcopal priest and author Barbara Brown Taylor notes, sin is collective; the systems do our sinning for us. That's why Micah confronts foreclosures by wealthy landowners who turn the poor out of their homes, because these are not just bad apples; they are propped up by a whole network of unjust laws that hit women and children the hardest.[20] As I write this, religious leaders are gathered in front of the nation's capital reading some of the more than two thousand Bible verses focused on poverty and justice, challenging the increasing impoverishment of millions of families and a national budget that increases economic inequality. Many of these faith leaders have been arrested for their witness.

Douglas Meeks, a United Methodist theologian and seminary professor, argues that our churches have blessed and baptized the culture's marketplace mentality. He writes,

> *The crisis for the Christian church in North America is that it has become too much absorbed into the market society in whose logic God's grace and God's justice cannot appear. The more the market logic threatens to become the church's way of organizing its life, the more the economy of the church is defined by the prevailing economy of our society and the more market rules determine what we mean by justice . . . The logic of accumulation and exchange invades every dimension of life. When this happens many persons are excluded from livelihood. "Surplus people," those who cannot be fit into the existing modes of production and consumption, are created . . . Theology should find its context among those whose freedom is denied by existing economic arrangements.*[21]

Over and over, theologians and disciples return to Jesus' preconditions for salvation for the wealthy man and they do so by looking hard at the economic systems of the world we find ourselves living in. Retired United Methodist bishop Kenneth Carder, in comments during a presentation on "Markets or Missions," joins this discipleship noting that the pervasive vision for ministry comes from market values of consumerism; the global market economy has become the dominant god of the modern world in opposition to the vulnerable, liberating, suffering God of the cross. Carder argues market values have been baptized and ritualized by the church and the gospel has become a commodity of self-interest, success, and national security. Wesley was clear, notes Carder, that wealth changes our logic and decreases our dependency on grace so that individual conversion is seen as more central to the gospel than shaping communities that are signs or foretastes of God's kin-dom. As a result, we define evangelism as that which finds a need and meets it rather than announcing God's reign and living it. When, Carder asks, do disciples become transformed by Jesus Christ, cross-bearing but risen?[22]

One of the ways John Wesley held on to that grace was by creating sewing collectives to provide work and income for impoverished people. He started lending collectives, through which the poor could find tools and materials needed to develop and sustain their own businesses. He created free health clinics as well as communal houses that were shared by women and children living in poverty and Methodist preachers, including himself. The hope was that communal living "liberates the privileged from blindness and the marginalized from invisibility."[23]

One place today we can see this radical discipleship that both recognizes our mutuality and fights to break free from the violent economic structures is in the Standing Rock movement. Standing Rock: the stunning and startling, huge and hopeful gathering of people fighting and praying for indigenous peoples' rights to land and water, as well as human rights and environmental justice. More than a thousand native people and their non-native allies created a nonviolent but militant movement to stop the Dakota Access Pipeline. Flying the flags of two hundred native nations from around the United States and Canada, the Red Warrior camp in southern North Dakota brought together tribes formerly identified as enemies; military veterans, who came to give other water protectors time to rest; and clergy and other religious leaders, calling on communities of faith to break the silence.

David Archambault II, former Standing Rock tribal chair, works to make visible the economic conditions and exploitations driving the water war. He writes:

> *When the Army Corps dammed the Missouri River in 1958, it took our riverfront forest, fruit orchards and most fertile farmlands. Now the Corps is taking our clean water and sacred places. Whether it's gold from the Black Hills or hydropower from the Missouri or oil pipelines that threaten our ancestral inheritance, the tribes have always paid the price for America's prosperity.*[24]

Against these economies of theft, Sabbath economics confronts the systems of injustice and creates alternatives. These alternatives are visible in the divestment campaigns as diverse as divestment from an apartheid South Africa to today's divestment from for-profit prison corporations. These divestment campaigns often draw folks together from across religious and political lines to find common ground. One campaign that has brought together environmental groups, racial justice organizations, labor organizers, immigrant and refugee coalitions, and religious and political groups from the left and right is the campaign against Nashville's Corrections Corporation of America. Corrections Corporation of America, the largest private prison corporation in the world, now renamed Civic Core, has created a new industry. By collaborating with the American Legislative Exchange Council (ALEC), Civic Core has been instrumental in pushing through new laws at national, state, and local levels to criminalize increasing numbers of impoverished black and brown people in order to make money. While Civic Core makes a profit each time they lock up somebody new, their "market growth" has also been a boon to everyone else making money from caging more folks. Bail, probation, parole, electronic monitoring and other forms of surveillance, video conference visits, commissary items, phone calls, and health care for those in prison are often handled by for-profit businesses whose monopoly on the market and entire business plan is to gouge people who have few choices and even fewer financial resources.

The ACLU begins an article asking, "What do the US Conference of Catholic Bishops, the Presbyterian Church USA, the United Methodist Church, the Episcopal Church, the Mennonite Central Committee, the Muslim Public Affairs Council, the Unitarian Universalist Association, and the United Church of Christ all have in common?" The answer: "They all agree that private prisons are a very, very bad idea." The United Methodist Church came out strong declaring its "opposition to the privatization of prisons and jails and to profit making from the punishment of human beings,"[25] but still, today, Civic Core's business analysts project future beds and earnings based on the demographics of our children.

Jesus tells the wealthy man: you must get rid of what you have, give it all away, and come and follow me. In this story, there is both withdrawal and renewal—a divestment from systems of oppression and investment in the kin-dom and Sabbath economies that know us as children of God. Salvation comes from the move away and the move towards. Salvation—as the women in the battered women's shelter knew and as the Standing Rock elders know—means we have to untangle ourselves from Caesar, from empire, from death-driving economies, and we have to become co-creators with God. We have to follow Jesus, welcoming the inbreaking of the kin-dom in our lives and our worlds. Withdrawal from the brutal and oppressive economic systems in order to seek justice and live into being alternative communities is not new and it is not over. It was visible from the earliest resistance movements to the enslavement of Africans and the impoverishment of indigenous peoples, in the Reconstruction era and in the civil rights movements, and can be seen now in economic cooperatives, credit unions, micro-lending, campaigns to provide living wages and equitable salaries, the fair trade movement, the Jubilee Campaign to forgive debt in third world nations, and moratoriums on new church buildings, pushing instead for investments in affordable housing.

Wahu Kaara, a Kenyan peacemaker and activist and executive director of the Kenya Debt Relief Network, spoke during the United Methodist Women's 2006 Assembly, declaring:

> *The greatest challenge in our pursuit of justice is to stand up and speak to power . . . We have commoditized our lives . . . When we let children die of treatable diseases, or make orphans because of inaccessible patented drugs denied to their folks for the sake of PROFIT, we are culpable in this betrayal. And this is sin, sin in the eyes of God! Life is no longer a manifestation of the Glory of God but a manifestation of Economic Might with the safeguards of the military industrial complex . . . We have sacrificed ourselves at the altar of money and earthly possessions . . . Today we women of the world must arise to the call. We must continue the nurturing and sustenance of life . . . We must with unflinching courage voice the concerns of injustice . . . We all must be determined because we must rebuild this world. A world of love, a world of partnership.*[26]

In the United Methodist Women's Mission Study book, *Latin America: People and Faith*, Brazilian author and journalist Sonia Maria Barbosa Dias argues that every congregation is to be a sign of the kin-dom of God. She elaborates, "... to proclaim the values of the kingdom and God's righteousness it is necessary to go in the opposite direction to all forms of individualism, consumerism, and social exclusion, working on all fronts of human dignity."[27] Following the Brazilian liberation theologian Leonardo Boff, she outlines the movement and possible process for this work, a communal movement that includes:

- a spiritual encounter among the crucified;
- an ethical outrage condemning an inhumane situation and call for action;
- a structural analysis of the mechanisms that create poverty and oppression;
- a critical judgment through the eyes of faith and reason;
- action led by those who are oppressed that effectively advances the process of liberation;
- a collective celebration of victories.[28]

United Methodist Women invite the church into this process, moving from immersion among those with their backs against the wall toward justice shaped by faith and concrete changes in systems of oppression. United Methodist Women members are rebuilding a world of partnership and love as they push for policies that reduce the income and wealth gap in the United States, stand with restaurant workers organizing for dignity and justice, partner with immigrants fighting against wage theft, and side with unpaid caregivers and low-wage workers fighting against economic exploitation. United Methodist Women supports Ministry with the Poor, one of the four focus areas of The United Methodist Church, an effort to move churches and conferences from programs and projects into authentic partnership with those who are impoverished. United Methodist Women collaborates with others in campaigns to expose and transform the economic injustices that impact women and children the hardest, especially women and children of color, and offers powerful resources on economic justice, noting the centrality of this work for all disciples of Jesus for the sake of our social and spiritual well-being.[29]

In *The Book of Resolutions of The United Methodist Church 2016*, we too commit to this work. "As a church," the resolution reminds us, "we are called to support the poor and challenge the rich . . . we emphasize measures that build and maintain the wealth of poor people, including asset-building strategies."[30] We frame the issues theologically, "[t]hat Jesus was born of a poor, unmarried woman who was living in a small nation, occupied and oppressed by a mighty foreign empire, concretely reveals God's full identification with poor, powerless, and oppressed people."[31] *The Book of Resolutions* provides rich material for congregations and communities to engage in discussions about what it means to live as the people of God here and now, recognizing that change is not easy, and that many will walk away grieving and sorrowful. However, echoing the words of Jesus in this story, while this challenge is most difficult, "for God all things are possible."

Mumia Abu-Jamal, a "prisoner of conscience," a black male political prisoner in an American prison who was for years confined to death row, has written numerous books and powerful poetry. I want to close this chapter with his poem.

Miracles

"Woe unto you that are rich, for ye have received your consolation" (Luke 6:24).

Not a god of thunder
a god of silk,
a god of the rich
did the carpenter speak,
but of a God of compassion,
of peace, of a day brighter
than today;
a God whose miracles still work
in the slave pens and shacks,
in the projects,
in the hellish daily life of the poor
and the oppressed—

Not miracles
like walking on waves,
transforming water into wine,
but miracles of love arising
in hearts where it seems least
likely to flourish—

here and there
in the *barrios* and the *favelas*,
among those who have least,
beat hearts of hope,
fly sparks of Overcoming.[32]

Personal Reflection:
Wrestling with Radical Discipleship

As you finish Mark 10, reflect in your journal about how might you, your congregation, and your community redefine or continue to redefine your practices to reflect Jesus' call into Sabbath economics? There is a powerful Hebrew word, *dayenu*, which is used in the Passover litany and means "more than enough" or "it would have been enough." The word reflects a theology of abundance, there is more than enough, which counters a theology of scarcity, there's never enough. God has provided more than enough and the distribution and redistribution of those resources is central to a Sabbath economics. What might it mean to examine your personal and congregational budget in light of this theology of abundance? How does your personal spending, your congregation's budget and use of resources, your community's budget, your nation's budget reflect or contradict the priorities of the kin-dom? And how might partnership with those with their backs most against the wall—a Sabbath economics partnership—"liberate the privileged from blindness and the marginalized from invisibility"?[33]

NOTES

ENDNOTES

1. Oscar Romero, *The Violence of Love: The Pastoral Wisdom of Archbishop Oscar Romero*, compiled and translated by James Brockman (San Francisco: Harper & Row, Publishers, 1988), 228.

2. Ibid, 157.

3. Ched Myers, *The Biblical Vision of Sabbath Economics* (Washington, D.C.: Tell the Word, 2002), 34.

4. Ibid., 33–34.

5. Alan Storey, "Radical Economic Transformation" (sermon, May 17, 2017, at Central Mission in Cape Town, South Africa). See Alan's website aslowwalk.org and his work with Manna and Mercy at mannaandmercy.org/alan-storey.html.

6. Carol Kuruvilla, "Christians Are More Likely to Say It's Poor People's Own Fault That They're Poor," *Huffpost Politics*, August 3, 2017, huffingtonpost.com/entry/christians-are-more-likely-to-say-its-poor-peoples-own-fault-that-theyre-poor_us_59833a3be4b00f0084ae61d6.

7. Ibid.

8. Peter Storey, "Re-Evangelizing the Church to Its Prophetic Ministry" (sermon, Methodists for Social Action Banquet, Ames, Iowa, June 11, 2005), 3–5.

9. Theodore W. Jennings Jr., *Good News to the Poor: John Wesley's Evangelical Economics* (Nashville: Abingdon Press, 1990), 107.

10. Ibid., 107–109.

11. Ibid., 105.

12. Bill Wylie-Kellerman, *Principalities in Particular: A Practical Theology of the Powers That Be* (Minneapolis: Fortress Press, 2017), 193–194.

13. Jennings, 136.

14. Ched Myers, Foreword in *The Biblical Jubilee and the Struggle for Life*, Ross Kinsler and Gloria Kinsler, ix.

15. James Lawson Jr., Foreword in *The Poverty and Justice Bible* (New York: American Bible Society, 1995).

16. Myers, *The Biblical Vision of Sabbath Economics*, 105.

17. Lee Camp, *Mere Discipleship: Radical Christianity in a Rebellious World* (Grand Rapids, MI: Brazos Press, 2003), 25.

18. Martin Luther King Jr., "The Current Crisis in Race Relations," in *A Testament of Hope: The Essential Writings of Martin Luther King, Jr.*, ed. James Melvin Washington (San Francisco: Harper & Row, Publishers, 1986), 89.

19. For a better understanding of what this looks like in the United States, read Douglas Blackmon's book, *Slavery by Another Name: The Re-Enslavement of Black Americans from the Civil War to World War II* (New York: Doubleday, 2008).

20. Barbara Brown Taylor, *Speaking of Sin: The Lost Language of Salvation* (Cambridge, MA: Cowley Publications, 2000), 65.

21. M. Douglas Meeks, *God the Economist: The Doctrine of God and Political Economy* (Minneapolis: Fortress Press, 1989), 37.

22. Author's notes from Ken Carder, "Markets or Missions" (lecture, Lake Junaluska, NC, n.d.).

23. Jennings, 59.

24. David Archambault II, "Taking a Stand at Standing Rock," *The New York Times*, August 24, 2016, nytimes.com/2016/08/25/opinion/taking-a-stand-at-standing-rock.html.

25. "Who is CCA? Numerous Religious Groups Condemn Prison Privatization," ACLU Tennessee, accessed June 4, 2018, aclu-tn.org/numerous-religious-groups-condemn-prison-privatization.

26. An article on Wahu Kaara's speech can be found here: Linda Bloom, "The Poor Also Have Dignity, Speakers Tell Women's Assembly," May 8, 2006, archives.gcah.org/bitstream/handle/10516/4999/article47.aspx.htm?sequence=1&isAllowed=y.

ENDNOTES *continued*

27. Sonia Maria Barbosa Dias, *Latin America: People and Faith* (New York: United Methodist Women, 2015), 97.

28. Ibid., 87.

29. "Economic Inequality," United Methodist Women, accessed May 30, 2018, unitedmethodistwomen.org/economic-inequality.

30. "The Economic Community," *The Book of Resolutions of The United Methodist Church 2016* (Nashville: The United Methodist Publishing House, 2016), 411.

31. "Global Economic Justice: The United Methodist Church, Food, Justice, and World Hunger," *The Book of Resolutions of The United Methodist Church 2016* (Nashville: The United Methodist Publishing House, 2016), 427.

32. Mumia Abu-Jamal, *Death Blossoms: Reflections from a Prisoner of Conscience* (Brooklyn: Litmus Books, 1996), 53–54.

33. Jennings, 62.

Chapter 5

Threatened with Resurrection: Mark 16:1–8

So they went out and fled from the tomb, for terror and amazement had seized them; and they said nothing to anyone, for they were afraid.
—Mark 16:8

Everyone baptized has received a share in Christ's prophetic mission.
—Oscar Romero, July 8, 1979[1]

If any want to become my followers, let them deny themselves and take up their cross and follow me.
—Mark 8:34

We should not wonder that a church has a great deal of cross to bear. Otherwise, it will not have much resurrection. An accommodating church, a church that seeks prestige without the pain of the cross, is not the authentic church of Jesus Christ.
—Oscar Romero, February 19, 1978[2]

Renew your church, Lord, your people in this land. Save us from cheap words and self-deception in your service. In the power of your Spirit transform us and shape us by your cross. Amen.
—John de Gruchy[3]

One of my favorite hymns, "Pass Me Not, O Gentle Savior," fills me with a passion that off-key introverts can only muster when a song that swallows our hearts catches us and something inside us explodes with a loud and resounding "Yes!" For me, it is this song of comfort and hope that offers an assurance that God is moving among us and would not pass us, pass me, by.

When I was about to leave my congregation in order to spend two months with base Christian communities and other churches in South Africa, I asked the congregation to sing this song as they sent me forth. The song felt like a prayer shawl, a wrapping around of powerful promises and accompaniment.

But when I returned two months later, when the congregation welcomed me home by singing "Pass Me Not," I felt myself grow smaller. Suddenly, in light of all I had seen and heard, experienced and encountered in South Africa, the song became more of a threat than a promise. I remembered the incredibly brave and fierce Christian communities I had stumbled into, the stories of brutality and unending hope, the holy boldness and fierce faith of being-resurrected-in-the-midst-of-death communities, and I was not so sure I was that brave. Maybe I wanted to be passed by.

I began to understand the original ending to Mark, and why later writers wanted more than the fearful, silent women as an Easter story. I began to understand why they, and we, work so hard to fix up these stories, to domesticate them, to end on a note of joy and celebration and not to end in terror. But Mark's author ends her story at verse eight—she wants us to feel the fear, to be caught in the terror and amazement, to reckon with what it means to know that the crucified has been raised and waits for us in the streets to pick up our cross and follow.

If Jesus raised does not simply mean life after death, if the resurrection pulls us back into the streets of Galilee where the Jesus movement began, if it pushes us back into conflict and persecution, surely we would feel both terror and amazement. If Jesus, crucified and raised, invites disciples into life in defiance of all the powers of death, into life that requires unmasking, naming, and engaging to transform powers and principalities, structures, systems, theologies, and institutionalized religion, might we not hope to be passed by?

Mark's version will not slide easily into most of our Easter celebrations. The author leaves no room for joyous choirs singing of streets paved in gold, for trumpets and organs accompanying triumphant hymns. She leaves no room for the parade of new clothes, large and lovely hats, huge blooming, sweet-scented lilies, chocolate candies, or Easter egg hunts. This Easter will not be contained in the stained-glass sanctuary. Instead, Mark pushes us into the streets and the struggles, where Jesus is out there waiting for us.

The women following Jesus into Galilee had been fierce and brave, providing for him on his journey. And they were there, standing at a distance, when Jesus was tortured and executed. All the male disciples fled, but the women remained (Mark 14:50; 15:40–41). They watched as Jesus was buried and the stone was moved to seal the tomb. And now at the end of Mark, they have come with spices to anoint Jesus' body. The women are startled when they discover his body is not there. The messenger recognizes their fear and tries to reassure them. The one who was crucified, the messenger tells them, has been raised and is already headed back to Galilee. That's where you'll find him.

Galilee, where the Jesus movement erupted, a poor people's movement rising up in defiance of all that justified and perpetuated suffering. It is in Galilee, where Jesus delivers his first sermon, calls disciples, creates community, confronts and destroys death-dealing powers, exposes religious lies and illusions, condemns religious leaders and the practices that rob people of life. And it is in Galilee, where Jesus provokes the anger of every group that holds power and privilege, where he teaches with authority in synagogues and the streets, identifies with and liberates those who are impoverished and oppressed, touches, cleanses, heals, affirms, commissions, ordains, embraces, forgives, includes, and loves fiercely those the world has labeled unclean, unwanted, unworthy, unlovable.

Easter in Mark is not simply spring out of winter, but it is an opposition to and subversion of the structures of power and privilege in the world. It is a manifesto, a clear declaration shouting that God's kin-dom comes in opposition to any religious, economic, political, and social structures that diminish life and threaten creation. And it is a kin-dom, kingdom, realm, rule, reign, and breaking into our world here and now with power over all the forms of death.

The cross, the crucifixion of Jesus, exposes in no uncertain terms this fierce clash, this fiery confrontation between empire and the kin-dom of God. Crucifixion in Jesus' time was a common form of torture and a reminder of the power of the state to define what would and would not be tolerated. Sometime near the time of Jesus' birth, more than two thousand peasants were crucified in Galilee for rebelling and left to die slowly along the road.[4] And this is where Jesus returned—Galilee. The trauma, the screams, the struggles of those nailed to their crosses were intended to solidify a sense of the Roman Empire's permanence and the peasants' powerlessness. Public crucifixions served as a warning to others who dared imagine a world freed from the systems of domination and empire, who dared to turn toward freedom. Crucifixion was meant to terrify and intimidate, to silence and sideline, to contain and control. The government held the power to crucify and used it often, targeting those identified as subversive, as enemies of the state.

Jesus was crucified. Not simply killed, but crucified. He was nailed to the cross under the sign, "King of the Jews," a title that belonged to Herod. His crucifixion was a public declaration of harsh retribution against anyone who might follow in his path. And radical discipleship, discipleship in Jesus' name, requires confrontation with these powers and principalities, with all that diminishes life, with ongoing crucifixions.

James Cone, a Pentecostal pastor and preacher, activist theologian, and seminary professor, is often referred to as the father of black liberation theology. Writing on what crucifixions look like today, he tells us:

> *Churches, seminaries and theological academies separated Christian identity from the horrendous violence committed against black people. Whites could claim a Christian identity without feeling the need to oppose slavery, segregation, and lynching as a contradiction of the gospel for America . . .*

> *Where is the gospel of Jesus' cross revealed today? The lynching of black America is taking place in the criminal justice system . . . One can lynch a person without a rope or tree.*[5]

A number of congregations are working hard to understand this and spend Good Friday moving from one site of crucifixion to another. They move from jails, prisons, sites where people with no shelter huddle in the night, to failing public schools, for-profit health care and prison corporations, discriminatory courts, to labor pools where people line up at five in the morning to wait to be chosen for day labor, paycheck loan businesses, pawn shops; they move to crumbling public housing projects, neighborhoods with densely concentrated poverty, cemeteries where the unnamed poor are buried in unmarked graves.

In 2017, a collaboration of organizations in Washington, D.C., created fourteen public interfaith Stations of the Cross, designed to provoke conversation about death-dealing systems and ongoing crucifixions. As one of the partners explains on their website:

> *Jesus walked the Via Dolorosa . . . Across the chasm of two thousand years, this tortured path resonates with current events for people of various faiths and backgrounds. Jesus' words upon the cross, "Why have you forsaken me?" speak acutely to the anguish and alienation felt by many today, from undocumented immigrants to religious, racial and ethnic minorities across our society.*[6]

The first station focused on the words, "Jesus is condemned to die." The artist, Ndume Olatushani, a teacher, organizer, and partner with the Children's Defense Fund's Nashville team, created a four-foot-by-nine-foot jail cell that mirrored the cell in which he often spent twenty-three hours a day for twenty years on death row—of a total of twenty-eight years he spent in prison—for a crime he did not commit. Ndume, a black man, was convicted by an all-white jury. He had never even been to the state in which the murder of a prominent white man was committed—until the police arrested him and took him there. It took the intervention of a team of advocates, including a large New York law firm, to finally secure Ndume's release from prison in June 2012.

His Stations of the Cross installation included wire bodies in orange jumpsuits, caged and leaning on the bars. There were three smaller bodies nearby: one in a child's school clothes, another a youth in a hoodie, and the third in an orange jumpsuit. Ndume brought to D.C. an art that insisted we confront the epidemic of black boys being pushed into prison. Interactive signs were posted near the exhibit, encouraging those who passed by to not only note their reaction to the information and art but their commitment to change the systems that continue to condemn people to death.

Ndume's installation was displayed on the grounds of the United Methodist General Board of Church and Society, directly across from the United States Supreme Court, as a visible challenge to the laws that continue to criminalize and abandon, condemn, and cage millions of people in this country. And the exhibit was an invitation to the church to recognize our compromise and complicity and to recommit ourselves to the God of Jesus and justice. As Ndume often notes, "All those years I was locked up, church folks came in trying to save my soul. Hell, I didn't need anyone to save my soul, I needed someone to save my ass."

Cone argues that we cannot separate the cross and the lynching tree, the cross and mass incarceration, false imprisonment, excessive sentencing, ongoing dehumanization. He argues that "[u]ntil we can see the cross and the lynching tree together, until we can identify Christ with a 'recrucified' black body hanging from a lynching tree, there can be no genuine understanding of Christian identity in America, and no deliverance from the brutal legacy of slavery and white supremacy."[7]

The following is something I often diagram when I am teaching and, while it is overly simplistic and dualistic, I include it here as a way to provoke deeper conversation about what it means to take up our cross and follow Jesus. It helps to start out with the question, "Why did Jesus die?" and then add, "Who killed Jesus?" Imagine responses from the communities around you, especially communities that are struggling for life. The urgent question in this context of radical discipleship is how the Jesus of Mark might respond.

Jesus was the only beloved son of God, fully divine, all knowing and all powerful, coming from heaven, royalty from the beginning.	**Jesus** was both fully human and divine; he was Jewish, born into an impoverished, oppressed, persecuted, militarily occupied, historically crucified peoples.
Jesus was **sent by God** to die on the cross, to save us from sin and death, and begin Christianity, the church.	Jesus was **sent by God** to show us the Way of Love, to disrupt and dismantle powers of death and call us into kin-dom living now.
The cross is the price God required to be paid for our sins; Jesus dies for our sins and because of our sins.	**The cross** is a direct consequence of Jesus' life and ministry, the response of the powers and principalities threatened by his ministry.
The crucifixion is a past event, over and done, not to be repeated.	**Crucifixions** are ongoing and disciples are those who follow in the way of the cross.
Sin is an individual moral failing. **Individuals make choices to break** covenant with God; this sin is seen most clearly in sexual immorality and murder.	**Sin** is both individual and collective; the **systems we uphold "do our sinning for us."** We see this in white supremacy, patriarchy, capitalism, and heterosexism.
Salvation is individual, a personal relationship with Jesus, recognized in a past moment of conversion.	**Salvation** is collective and ongoing, requiring both a personal and collective conversion, day after day.
Belief is confirmed by our profession of faith.	**Belief** is confirmed by our risky, radical, embodied, cross-bearing discipleship.

continued on page 124

continued from page 123

Baptism is a sign of being saved and a requirement for church membership and salvation; for children it is a sign of parental commitment to raise the child in the church.	**Baptism** is confirmation of our willingness to pick up our cross and follow Jesus day after day; for children, it is confirmation of the congregation's commitment to live in a way that reminds them of who and whose they are.
Ministry is focused on converting individuals to a profession of faith so that they might also be saved.	**Ministry** is focused on building Beloved Community as a sign of God's kin-dom and militant, nonviolent, anti-death movements.
Allegiance to Jesus requires church membership, active attendance in church activities, and is not seen as being incompatible with the status quo.	**Allegiance to Jesus** requires collective confrontation with the powers of death and a refusal to cooperate with the systems of domination, the status quo.
Church prepares us for heaven after we die and for living well now; religion has nothing to do with politics; God has ordained the way things are.	**Church** prepares us for abundant life here and now, and for engaging systems and structures of death; it is impossible to be apolitical if you are a Christian; the way of the world is not the way God wants it to be.
Worship is meant to comfort and console, to inspire and encourage, to remind us of the life that is yet to come.	**Worship** is meant to resurrect a Jesus-movement people, exposing our complicity, renewing our courage to confront powers of death-dealing systems and theologies.
Communion is an individual act of repentance and reconciliation with Christ; we express regret for individual moral failures and are comforted by assurance of forgiveness.	**Communion** is a collective act naming systemic and individual sin, and reviving the being-resurrected, anti-death community to be reconcilers with God and neighbor.

This first interpretation of the cross invites people into a faith that has little if any impact on the systems and structures of death—on economic exploitation and perpetual impoverishment, on sexism and heterosexism, on militarism and other forms of systemic violence, on xenophobia and white privilege, on white supremacy and plantation capitalism.[8] The communion call to "[d]o this in remembrance of me" becomes a remembering of Jesus' death that saves us and assures our afterlife, but does not require radical change here and now, and most surely does not require confrontation with empires.

In the second interpretation, however, cross bearing is required of all disciples. The only time the term "remembrance" is used in Mark is in 14:9, the story of the unnamed woman who anoints Jesus. I opened this study with that scripture, in remembrance of this woman who broke through the barriers of a patriarchal world, through the closed minds of the male disciples in order to anoint Jesus. And in breaking through, she recognized what the male disciples refused to see: Jesus, the Messiah, Beloved of God, the Anointed One would be crucified, for she understood crucifixion is the direct consequence of the proclamation and practice of the kin-dom of God. Theodore Jennings notes that this woman is the "only apostle of the crucified."[9] Hisako Kinukawa writes in *Women and Jesus in Mark: A Japanese Feminist Perspective* that this story would have been dangerous for the early church. "The anointing woman became a destructive, unacceptable, and irrational barrier-breaker, putting herself into a life-and-death struggle in solidarity with Jesus' struggle."[10] Remembrance here is bold, fierce, convicted; remembrance here reminds us that each one of us is called to bear the cross.

Communion that mirrors Mark's story becomes an ongoing part of the story of liberation. The context is Passover, the annual Jewish celebration of God's deliverance. In the Passover ritual, families gather to remind their children why this day is holy: once we were caught in the web of oppression, slaves in bondage to Pharaoh's empire, but God took sides and delivered us. God the Liberator set us free. The Exodus is a liberating movement continued by the prophets and embodied by Jesus. In this context, communion becomes a source of communal power, a liturgical act that resurrects, that calls back into life a community of resistance.

It reminds us of our baptism. When James and John plead with Jesus to be rewarded by sitting on his right and left hand in glory, Jesus asks, "Are you able to drink this cup that I drink, or be baptized with the baptism that I am baptized with?" (Mark 10:35–40). Jesus refers here to the cross, reminding the disciples during the Last Supper that the cup is his blood. In the Garden of Gethsemane, Jesus, "distressed and agitated," prays to God to "remove this cup from me" (Mark 14:33, 36).

Drinking the cup, being baptized with this baptism, is the sign that disciples are willing to pick up their cross and follow. And this commitment is echoed in our baptismal vows in which we commit to renouncing the evil powers of this world. And we commit to affirming the power God gives us "to resist evil, injustice, and oppression in whatever forms they present themselves."[11] We do so because Jesus Christ, not Caesar or any form of Caesar, is Lord; God's reign is the only kin-dom, kingdom, the only empire, to which we pledge our allegiance, our lives. Communion then is a recommitment to our cross-bearing discipleship, a reminder that our baptismal vows must be embodied day after day.

As Theodore Jennings writes:

> *This resurrection is the "uprising," the insurrection, of one who rejected the rules of respectability, the religious laws, the institutions of family and church and state. It is the resurrection of the one who provoked these structures, enraged them and was condemned by them . . . the structures and institutions that rejected and condemned him are themselves exposed as the enemies of God. The structures of piety, of morality, of liturgy of law and order, of nation and empire—these crumble now before the message of the uprising of the crucified . . . This is by no means a consoling word but a profoundly disturbing and challenging one . . . a shattering force . . . it isn't over. It's about to begin.*[12]

"It isn't over. It's about to begin." The question then becomes, how do we break through the silence and fear in order to practice resurrection? How do we create and sustain being-resurrected communities committed to following Jesus in the Way of the Cross?

The good news is that Jesus does not give up on us even when we give up on the Way of the Cross, on radical discipleship. The three women stand in stark contrast to Peter, James, and John, the male disciples who betrayed and denied Jesus, who abandoned him and fled. And yet they too will become a part of the being-resurrected community.

Being partners with and being held accountable by communities that are the targets of unjust systems and theologies often creates the courage needed to resist death and domination, and creates space for all our healing. It is my hope in returning again and again to the lessons of radical discipleship in Mark—in prisons, in churches, on the streets, and now, with you, in this book—that we will find creative ways to form community and long-term, authentic, and mutual relationships with those who are pushed to the margins by the systems and structures, by the theologies and institutions of domination.

I am a partner in the Community Building and Conflict Resolution Circle on Tennessee's death row. It is an incredibly powerful group of men who practice resurrection on a daily basis. Several of the men have come within hours of execution and were at the last minute moved off of deathwatch back into their cells and solitary confinements. When we started the group in 2012, the men said they wanted to learn more about building community, resolving conflict, and practicing nonviolence. In the belly of the beast, the harshest portion of the prison system, these men chose to build an alternative community, believing that love would have the last word. In a group of men who had so rarely known love, the community became a visible source of love and hope. Every gathering starts with an opening circle and meditation, a time of sharing celebrations and struggles. And every gathering ends with a closing circle, for the men are committed to the circle process. And they are committed to loving, in defiance of the world in which they are forced to live, in contradiction to their childhoods, which were by and large brutal and without love, in spite of the labels the world has given them. One of the men noted that he was almost seventy years old and it was not until he became a part of this circle that he stumbled into love, real love.

The men have written to young people who are struggling. These are not scared-straight letters, but letters that say, "I know what it is to feel like a piece a trash on the side of the road that no one notices." Their booklet of letters was specifically written for a group of young black and brown high school youth struggling with school and the streets. The booklet begins with a quote from Aboriginal activists in Queensland, Australia: "If you have come to help me, you are wasting your time. But if you have come because your liberation is bound up with mine, then let us work together."[13]

And then the men wrote directly to the young folks. They wrote, "We have been where you are, we know so many of the hurts you have experienced, so many of the struggles you are going through, and we want to work with you, to talk with you, to accompany you so that you might live to be really, fully you, fully alive, here and now." The men explained that they had thought hard about how to let the young people know that they were listening, really listening, that they were thinking about all the struggles the young folks were going through, all the people who "write you off, dismiss you or make you think you don't matter." When the group was trying to reach consensus on the most important part of this work, they decided it was a three-word question: "Are you okay?"

"We thought about how so many community systems fail you and make life harder for you when they should be providing support. We thought about how angry and hurt you must feel about all the ways in which you have experienced violence and push out, exclusion and put downs, racism and poverty, wounds and heartaches." They wanted the young people to know they were willing to love them into new life.

Abu Ali Abdur'Rahman, a member of our circle who was severely battered and abused, tortured and terrified as a child, once came within hours of execution. At the time he wrote his letter for the booklet, he was once again on a list of next to be executed. Many of us are convinced he is innocent of the crime he was accused of and convicted for, and we hope he becomes part of the more than ten men we have worked with whose sentences were overturned or redefined and released from death row. Abu wrote, "We have a challenge, you and I . . . Love must be retrieved, revived and restored. It behooves us to take our rightful place at the table as first-class citizens."

Pervis, another member of the group, notes, "As my dad used to say, just a simple old-man statement, 'We blowing back the trash to get a drink of water.' And that's what we're doing. We may not be able to go on the outside, but we're being heard; we're doing inner-Freedom Rides, making something happen."

Members of this Community Building and Conflict Resolution Circle on death row completed more than forty hours of training on mediation and conflict management, the same training required by the Tennessee Supreme Court for those seeking to be qualified as court-approved mediators. They created a mediation process that has been approved by the administration and is resolving disputes between insiders on death row and between insiders and correctional officers. They have been successful, repeatedly, teaching other insiders and correctional officers alternatives for managing conflict. They are now teachers for the next eight men who have signed up to take the course, working with professors and certified mediators to change the culture on death row. They are practicing resurrection, day after day betting everything on life and refusing to be defined by the powers and systems of death.

Junot Diaz, Dominican-American Pulitzer Prize–winning author, argues that in the face of death and systems of death, "radical hope is our best weapon." Diaz quotes philosopher Jonathan Lear, who says, "What makes this hope radical is that it is directed toward a future goodness that transcends the current ability to understand what it is." And then Diaz continues, "Radical hope is not so much something you have but something you practice."[14]

The women with Jesus are terrified and amazed. Terrified of the crosses that await, the call back into the streets of Galilee, the radicality of discipleship in Jesus' name. For a moment fear silences them. But they are also caught up in awe—astonished, amazed, stunned by the reality of the resurrection, the power of God over all other powers in their lives, all the powers of death. And Mark leaves the story hanging in that moment, waiting for the response of her readers. Having encountered this loving, liberating, healing, animating, confrontational, fierce, defiant, life-giving, and world-transforming Jesus, crucified and raised, how will we respond?

Like the women, I suspect most of us hear this invitation as both a promise and perhaps a threat, both with hope and terror, with awe and fear. Jesus, crucified and raised, is powerfully present among us and waiting for our response.

In Nicaragua, during the Contra War, base Christian communities gathered to respond. They gathered to call out the names of those killed in state-sanctioned violence, claiming the power of resurrection in defiance of the powers of death. As each name was called out, the community shouted, "*¡Presente!*" Present—here, now, among us; not gone, not forgotten, but here with the power to encourage and challenge, here with the power to stir us up and call us into repentance and resistance. *¡Presente!* Here to accompany us in the struggle for life, as the poet Julia Esquivel writes in the concluding poem in this chapter.

And so it is with Jesus. Jesus, present and waiting for us in the very streets where the powers still destroy life—in the parking lot of the prison on a snowy Christmas Eve, in the cages of solitary confinement on death row, in the streets of Ferguson and in housing projects across the nation, in the mountains of Nicaragua, and the cities of South Africa and Liberia. Jesus, present and accompanying us on this journey—not confined to some faraway heaven but here, now, among us, calling us into radical discipleship. Calling us into the kind of discipleship we encounter in base Christian communities and twelve-step programs, in the Movement for Black Lives, and in the water protectors at Standing Rock. Jesus, *¡Presente!* Jesus, challenging our biases and assumptions, walking with us through fears and doubts, encouraging us as we embody Beloved Community and sustain being-resurrected-on-the-journey congregations. Jesus *¡Presente!* Jesus, with us in the healing circle on death row and in Children's Defense Fund Freedom Schools. Jesus, waiting for us in the streets, reminding us that charity is not enough and nothing less than a redistribution of power and privilege, wealth and resources is required. Jesus, calling to us, challenging us: in the witness of Fayette and Roger, Ndume and Joseph, in a child's prayer and a mother's plea, along the border with Bishop Carcaño and in safe houses with Susan Burton. Jesus *¡Presente!* Jesus, inviting us to give flesh to Sabbath economics and kin-dom living, disrupting and dismantling, challenging and changing the systems and structures, theologies and institutions that prop up racism and xenophobia, sexism and heterosexism, militarism and materialism, empire and economic exploitation, marketplace mentalities and greed. Jesus *¡Presente!* Jesus, crucified and raised, continuing to walk with us in the movements for justice and joy, generosity and grace, freedom and faith, liberation and life. *¡Presente!* Jesus, among us, inviting us to bet everything, all that we have and all that we are, on God's truth: Love wins! Jesus *¡Presente!*

In the words of exiled Guatemalan poet Julia Esquivel from her book *Threatened with Resurrection:*

They Have Threatened Us with Resurrection

. . . What keeps us from sleeping
is that they have threatened us with Resurrection!
Because every evening
though weary of killings,
an endless inventory since 1954,
yet we go on loving life
and do not accept their death!

They have threatened us with Resurrection
because we have felt their inert bodies
and their souls penetrated ours
doubly fortified.
Because in this marathon of Hope,
there are always others to relieve us
who carry the strength
to reach the finish line
which lies beyond death.

They have threatened us with Resurrection
because they will not be able to take away from us
their bodies,
their souls,
their strength,
their spirit,
nor even their death
and least of all their life.
Because they live
today, tomorrow, and always
on the streets, baptized with their blood
and in the air that absorbed their cry . . .

. . . They have threatened us with Resurrection,
because they are more alive than ever before,
because they transform our agonies,
and fertilize our struggle,
because they pick us up when we fall,
because they look like giants
before the crazed gorillas' fear . . .

. . . That is the whirlwind
which does not let us sleep,
the reason why asleep, we keep watch,
and awake, we dream . . .

. . . it is the earthquake soon to come
that will shake the world
and put everything in its place . . .

. . . Join us in this vigil
and you will know what it is to dream!
Then you will know how marvelous it is
to live threatened with Resurrection!

To dream awake,
to keep watch asleep,
to live while dying,
and to know ourselves already
resurrected![15]

Personal Reflection: Wrestling with Radical Discipleship

I was preparing for our Good Friday services one year and decided to walk outside to see if someone had included the service time on our sign. A woman walked by, someone I knew was mostly living under a nearby bridge, and asked, "What's all this about?" So, I explained Good Friday, or tried to—the cross before the resurrection, the death before new life, the importance of not just rushing into Easter but spending time at the foot of the cross, a reminder of the powers of death at work in our world. "I don't know too many people who need reminding about death showing up on every corner. Know lots who could use a reminder about the getting up part, about maybe living for real."

The Book of Discipline of The United Methodist Church states,

> *With other Christians we recognize that the reign of God is both a present and future reality. The church is called to be that place where the first signs of the reign of God are identified and acknowledged in the world. Wherever persons are being made new creatures in Christ, wherever the insights and resources of the gospel are brought to bear on the life of the world, God's reign is already effective in its healing and renewing power.*[16]

How might your congregation become a "place where the first signs of the reign of God are identified?" Examine the hymns, songs, litanies, prayers, sermons, and Bible studies used in your congregation, taking notes over at least a two- to three-week period. What meaning do they give to the cross and resurrection? How do they reflect Jesus' insistence that disciples must pick up our crosses and follow in his path, consistently confronting the systems and structures, theologies and institutions that perpetuate domination and oppression? How are the voices, stories, values, and decisions of those pushed until their backs are against the wall included or excluded, privileged, or silenced? In what ways might your congregation, your community, become a signpost of the inbreaking kin-dom of God? How will you practice resurrection?

ENDNOTES

1. Oscar Romero, *The Violence of Love: The Pastoral Wisdom of Archbishop Oscar Romero*, compiled and translated by James Brockman (San Francisco: Harper & Row Publishers, 1988), 173.
2. Ibid., 43.
3. John de Gruchy, *Cry Justice! Prayers, Meditations and Readings from South Africa* (Maryknoll, NY: Orbis Books, 1986), 181.
4. Obery Hendricks Jr., *The Politics of Jesus: Rediscovering the True Revolutionary Nature of Jesus' Teachings and How They Have Been Corrupted* (New York: Doubleday, 2006), 51.
5. James Cone, *The Cross and the Lynching Tree* (Maryknoll, NY: Orbis Books, 2011), 159, 163.
6. "Stations of the Cross," Coexist House, accessed August 31, 2017, coexisthouse.org.uk/stations-2017.html.
7. Cone, xv.
8. "Plantation capitalism" is a term that is often used by Rev. James Morris Lawson Jr., architect of the nonviolent civil rights movement in the United States, a colleague of Dr. Martin Luther King's, and a United Methodist pastor.
9. Theodore W. Jennings Jr., *The Insurrection of the Crucified: The "Gospel of Mark" as Theological Manifesto* (Chicago: Exploration Press, 2003), 241.
10. Hisako Kinukawa, *Women and Jesus in Mark: A Japanese Feminist Perspective* (Maryknoll, NY: Orbis Books, 1994), 89.
11. "The Baptismal Covenant I: Renunciation of Sin and Profession of Faith" in *The United Methodist Hymnal* (Nashville: The United Methodist Publishing House, 1989), 34.
12. Jennings, 309–310.
13. "Lilla Watson," Revolvy, accessed June 10, 2017, topics.revolvy.com/topic/Lilla%20Watson. Lilla Watson is said to have offered this comment during her speech in Nairobi at the United Nations Decade for Women Conference in 1985. However, she has declined credit for the quote, arguing that it came from a collective process by Aboriginal activists in Queensland, Australia, in the 1970s.

ENDNOTES *continued*

14. Junot Díaz, " Under President Trump, Radical Hope Is Our Best Weapon," *The New Yorker*, November 21, 2016, newyorker.com/magazine/2016/11/21/under-president-trump-radical-hope-is-our-best-weapon. Diaz was accused by two women of making unwanted sexual advances. After an investigation, MIT retained him as a professor and the *Boston Review* also retained him as one of their editors. I wholeheartedly support the #MeToo movement and those who have the courage to tell their stories. Including his words here is not an endorsement of any harmful behavior.

15. Julia Esquivel, *Threatened with Resurrection: Prayers and Poems from an Exiled Guatemalan* (Elgin, IL: The Brethren Press, 1994), 59–65.

16. *The Book of Discipline of The United Methodist Church 2016,* ¶102 (Nashville: The United Methodist Publishing House, 2016), 50.

Postscript

Becoming Beloved Community, Practicing Resurrection

Where can I come and see what you believe?
—Gary Gunderson[1]

The church is never more true than when it remembers its origin as a sect, a minority opinion, a countercultural, antiestablishment movement; questioning the rightness of things as they are has again and again been the spark of the church's renewal and a hallmark of its faithfulness to the gospel.
—David Rensberger[2]

Courage, dear friends I know for many the hour of testing has come and they have fled as cowards; catechists, celebrants of the word, people who shared with us the joys of our meetings, have been frightened. People we thought very strong are frightened away because they have forgotten that this is a religion of life. And, as life, it must clash with the life that is not God's life but exists as the kingdom of darkness and of sin in the world.
—Oscar Romero, October 29, 1978[3]

The church has been reborn time and again whenever it has remembered that it is first and foremost a movement for radical personal and political transformation accountable to God's dream of justice and shalom.
—Ched Myers[4]

Who do you say Christ is by the way you live? Who do we say Christ is by the way we live? . . . Is there an alleluia deep inside you growing rusty? Awake and stand in the light. Praise God's name with singing and dancing! Unbutton yourselves and stand open to catch the wind. May they say of us: They are drunk on new wine . . . the new wine of the Spirit.
—Ann Weems[5]

My friend, mentor, and colleague Hogan was the pastor of a downtown congregation in Nashville until he joined in a protest against the assassination of Archbishop Oscar Romero by a military-backed death squad. After Hogan helped to carry a casket through downtown, protesting the U.S. training and financing of death squads in El Salvador, the execution of Romero, and the ongoing collaboration by American empire in systemic violence around the globe, Hogan's congregation suggested it was time for him to retire. Hogan was unflustered, remarking that being a prophet was a permanent job. He immediately had cards made up with his contact information and the title, "Consultant on Resurrection." He was a partner in the first team of Witness for Peace in Nicaragua during the Contra War, standing with others to confront and stop the violence. Knowing the reality and horror of death, Hogan practiced and lived the joy of resurrection.

When we had meetings, Hogan would bring photos of the murdered priests and their housekeeper in El Salvador, reminding us what our tax dollars make possible and probable.[6] But Hogan was also the first to invite us to dance. As soon as a meeting was over, Hogan would begin smiling and ask, "So where will we dance tonight?" And Hogan danced. At six feet four inches he was a sight to behold—arms and legs going in all directions, he danced with absolute delight and utter disregard for folks watching his unique form.

In a worship service with a base Christian community in Nicaragua, Hogan struggled to catch all the words of the sermon. His hearing had diminished and his Spanish was less than fluent but he could pick up the main pieces. In response to the preaching, Hogan would holler, "*A la lucha!*" meaning "to the struggle": to the struggle for justice and liberation, to the struggle for freedom and transformation. The Nicaraguan pastor was in fact saying, "Alleluia!" Several folks tried to alert Hogan to his inaccurate translation but he could not hear and they gave up. Repeatedly Hogan waved his hand shouting, "*A la lucha*, amen!" After the service was over, several people explained to Hogan about his misunderstanding. Hogan was unfazed, saying: "One and the same! *A la lucha* is Alleluia! And Alleluia is *a la lucha*! To struggle for justice is always to praise the God who is already at work among us; and alleluia, to glorify God, to give God thanks, is always to join God in the struggle for justice!"

Nelson and Joyce Johnson are, like Hogan, steeped in the struggles for justice and in the joy of resurrection. They are gentle and generous, fierce and fiery in their leadership with the Beloved Community Center and Faith Community Church in Greensboro, North Carolina, where Nelson serves as pastor. Beloved Community Center seeks to model the vision and spirit of Dr. Martin Luther King Jr. and Ella Baker[7] by putting flesh on organizing nonviolent direct action. They work on a wide variety of struggles, including civic engagement and democratic justice, truth and reconciliation, police accountability, and economic justice. Their vision for justice is rooted in their gospel faith, in their radical discipleship, and in their willingness to follow in the way of this crucified and raised Jesus.

The commitment of Beloved Community creates collaborative work "toward social and economic relations that affirm and realize the equality, dignity, worth, and potential of every person."[8] Their creative courage and relentless grace provide glimpses of the kin-dom among us as they engage gang members as leaders for transforming communities, college students in uncovering and documenting grassroots history, workers in challenging and changing unjust labor practices and inadequate wages, pastors in reimagining church, organizers in the Moral Monday movement, and communities in seeking truth.

They have a long history of practicing resurrection, nurturing and sustaining a being-resurrected-on-the-journey community of faith, engaging the powers and principalities of death in the name of the Lord of Life. Both Nelson and Joyce are partners in the National Council of Elders, elders of the civil rights movements, and nonviolent practitioners during the twentieth and twenty-first centuries. On

November 3, 1979, Nelson was leading a protest against economic exploitation and white supremacy in a housing project in Greensboro, North Carolina. A caravan of cars loaded with members of the American Nazi Party and the Ku Klux Klan arrived and opened fire, killing five of the demonstrators and wounding ten, including Nelson. While the protestors had a parade permit and the police knew of their gathering and had been warned about the possible attack by the white supremacists, there was no police intervention. Four television film crews were present and documented the shootings. Twice those identified as shooters were acquitted of wrongdoing by state and federal courts.

Joyce and Nelson were primary organizers behind the creation of the Greensboro Truth and Reconciliation Commission, the first truth and reconciliation commission to be held in the United States. Over a period of two years, with help from members of South Africa's Truth and Reconciliation Commission (TRC), Greensboro's TRC heard testimony, studied files and documents, and convened public forums. Almost thirty years after the massacre, the commission held three public hearings on the following topics: what created the conditions for the events of November 3, 1979; what actually happened on that day and why; what has been the ongoing impact of the trauma and terror, the injustices and silence, on the community; and how might the city move toward healing and hope.[9] In the last months of 2017, almost forty years after the murders, the Greensboro City Council issued an apology for the city's role in the events.[10]

Kathy Sanchez, a leader among indigenous women in the Pueblos of the Southwestern United States, a healer fluent in her mother tongue, Tewa, and a member of the National Council of Elders, founded Tewa Women United, emphasizing that indigenous peoples must:

> *. . . recognize the historical context and trauma that has continued to have enormous repercussions through our generation. We needed to understand and heal from the impact—biological, social and economic—that the heritage of conquest, forced assimilation and loss of culture and language, has on us as people . . . In the safe space we created, we transformed and empowered one another . . . by embracing and reaffirming our cultural identity.*[11]

"*Wi don gi mu*," in Tewa, may be translated as "we are one," in mind, heart, and in the spirit of love for all. And it is in this spirit of love that Kathy and others created SaYain, the Circle of Grandmothers, that brings the Tewa language and culture, stories, and songs to the younger generations, rooting them in their identity as strong women with the power to change their communities "so that our children and our culture can truly thrive . . . Together we heal, connect, and grow beloved communities."[12] Tewa Women United speak of *wo watsi*, "the path of life [that] follows into our daily work,"[13] the path that leads to life and shapes our day-after-day living and loving. We must root ourselves in love, reconnect with the earth and with our ancestors, she argues; we must recognize the sacred worth of all living beings and the necessity of interdependence.

Resurrection was what I saw in the transformation and ongoing conversion of the Hobson congregation. Over and over again, an inbreaking of the kin-dom occurred as we struggled to be faithful disciples. I remember a moment during baptisms one Easter morning: A young man, living on the streets, struggling with crack addiction and deep depression, hurting from old wounds of abuse and neglect, had gone through our new member class to come to this moment. As he turned to face the congregation, tears streaming down his face, he whispered, "I always thought you had to die to get to heaven. But here it is, all I've ever wanted: a family that claims me, a place where I belong."

Jesus calls us into radical discipleship here and now, inviting us into partnership with the God who is making all things new. This is not easy for disciples, then or now, for though we are called to be change agents, we most often resist change as fiercely as the world around us.

As I write this postscript, women across the world are breaking generations of silence and joining the #MeToo movement, a growing witness by women confronting those in power who have harassed and assaulted them over the years. Initiated by Tarana Burke, a black organizer and activist from the Bronx in New York City, the movement has gained momentum and visibility. #MeToo witnesses include celebrities and maids, journalists and secretaries, political aids and college students, corporate interns and fieldworkers, immigrants and lawyers. The individual stories unmask the easy assurances of identifying a few problematic individuals, and instead, push us to collectively challenge the culture of patriarchy and sexual violence, and the institutions and theologies that support them.

For generations, United Methodist Women has unmasked sexual violence and patriarchy, and may have helped awaken more communities to this movement with the "Airing Dirty Laundry" exhibit during the 2014 Assembly, an exhibit that publicly displayed images and stories of violence against women. United Methodist Women has created resources, equipped and mobilized congregations, and initiated advocacy efforts such as "I Believe You" and "Am I My Sister's Keeper?" One of the United Methodist Women's initiatives against sexual violence reports that "eighty-five percent of confirmed sex trafficking victims in the world are in the United States, and most of them are runaway children." United Methodist Women has exposed and confronted those complicit with the systems that perpetuate sexual violence, stood with women and children who have been trafficked, insisting that this witness and work is essential in living out our faith.

I offer these stories and this study as an open-ended encounter with Mark's Gospel and the world. While I have lifted up moments and movements, glimpses of what radical discipleship might mean, I have resisted prescribing "right response," insisting that the journey is ongoing for all of us. We are, day after day, liberated by the God of life, set free by the crucified and resurrected Nazarene, so that we might be partners with God in the ongoing work of liberation, freedom, and salvation in the world.

In Mark 7:9, Jesus challenges a group of Pharisees and scribes, insisting, "You have a fine way of rejecting the commandment of God in order to keep your tradition!" I hear these words as an unmasking of the ways in which I have traded God's call into the hard work of radical discipleship for the comfortable traditions of my social location, my church, my community, and my nation. I hear it as an invitation to be set free once again, day after day, from all the powers that seek my silence and complicity. And I sink into the invitation of Dorothee Soelle, practicing amazement, unlearning, and letting go, resisting in order to heal, healing in order to resist.

When a scribe in Mark 12 asks Jesus what the greatest commandment is, Jesus responds with the Shema prayer, the heart of the Jewish faith and ours: we must love God with all that we are and all that we have, and love all others, as we learn to love ourselves in the light of God's gracious, generous, extravagant, never-ending love. After the man's lengthy agreement that this is indeed the greatest commandment, Jesus declares, "You are not far from the kingdom of God" (Mark 12:28–34).

The ongoing journey of radical discipleship pulls us toward the kin-dom of God and releases us for life abundant, outrageous hope, and deep and abiding joy. We are loved into life and invited to spill that life-giving, boundary-breaking, world-transforming love into the world around us. It is not easy. As Brian Andreas, artist and storyteller, writes, "Anyone can slay a dragon . . . but try waking up every morning and loving the world all over again. That's what takes a real hero."[14]

The shorter ending of Mark ends at verse 8, waiting for us to wake up and love the world all over again, prodding us to move into the streets where Jesus waits. We know from other stories in the Bible that the women disciples in these stories from Mark moved through their fear and silence, spilling into the streets of Galilee, embodying love, practicing resurrection, persisting as partners in this being-saved-on-the-journey community of radical disciples.

Vincent Harding, historian, nonviolent prophet, and the author of much of Dr. King's April 4, 1967, "Beyond Vietnam" speech, created the Veterans of Hope Project, a project that includes interviews with civil rights movement partners. Just as there are veterans of war who are honored, Harding argued, there are veterans of hope, peace, and justice—those who have struggled to make this world more loving, more just, more like kin-dom—who should be recognized and celebrated. One of the veterans of hope is Gwendolyn Zoharah Simmons, activist and college professor, a partner in Student Nonviolent Coordinating Committee (SNCC) and the 1964 Mississippi Freedom Summer. Zoharah remembers walking the streets of Laurel, Mississippi, and knocking on doors, trying to find people who might be supportive in the work to register black voters and challenge the ongoing terrorism of lynchings and Jim Crow. She remembers an older black woman answering her knock, opening the door, listening to her explanation about working with freedom-seeking organizations. The older woman held open her door saying, "Girl, I've been waiting on you all my life. Come on in."[15]

The world waits for the church to really be the church, to embody love, practice resurrection, to put flesh on a faith you can see. Dr. Martin Luther King Jr. wrote, "love without power is sentimental and anemic. Power at its best is love implementing the demands of justice, and justice at its best is power correcting everything that stands against love."[16] Cornel West, philosopher and theologian, professor inside prisons and seminaries, summarizes this, arguing, "Justice is what love looks like in public."[17]

I would like to close with the words of Emilie Townes, a womanist theologian, poet, and dean of Vanderbilt Divinity School, who writes in *Breaking the Fine Rain of Death* a blessing and benediction of hope and freedom, an invitation and prophetic demand that includes these words:

> *. . . hope reminds us that we cannot accept the death-dealing and life-denying ways in which we have often structured our existences . . . all who hope in Christ have accepted a gift that will always challenge and always change us . . . we are set free to serve and free others, with full hearts—we can do this . . .*[18]

ENDNOTES

1. Gary Gunderson, *Deeply Woven Roots: Improving the Quality of Life in Your Community* (Minneapolis: Fortress Press, 1997), 85.

2. David Rensberger, *Johannine Faith and Liberating Community* (Philadelphia: The Westminster Press, 1988), 136.

3. Oscar Romero, *The Violence of Love: The Pastoral Wisdom of Archbishop Oscar Romero*, compiled and translated by James Brockman (San Francisco: Harper & Row, Publishers, 1988), 117.

4. Ched Myers, "What Is Radical Discipleship?" Radical Discipleship, March 5, 2015, radicaldiscipleship.net/2015/03/05/what-is-radical-discipleship.

5. Ann Weems, *Reaching for Rainbows: Resources for Creative Worship* (Louisville: Westminster John Knox Press, 1980), 99.

6. On November 16, 1989, a Salvadoran death squad came on to the campus of the Universidad Centroamericana in San Salvador, El Salvador, and executed six Jesuit priests, their housekeeper, and her daughter. The priests were U.S. citizens supporting movements to challenge structural injustices and challenging the political and financial support of the United States for the death squads and economic exploitation. See nytimes.com/1989/11/17/world/6-priests-killed-in-a-campus-raid-in-san-salvador.html and washingtonpost.com/wp-srv/WPcap/1999-11/16/049r-111699-idx.html.

7. Ella Baker was a key nonviolent organizer working with voter registration, providing leadership with the Southern Christian Leadership Conference, and facilitating the founding of the Student Nonviolent Coordinating Committee. For more on her radical, womanist, indigenous practices of leadership see Barbara Ransby's *Ella Baker and the Black Freedom Movement: A Radical Democratic Vision* (Chapel Hill: University of North Carolina Press, 2003).

ENDNOTES *continued*

8. Beloved Community Center, home page, accessed August 5, 2017, belovedcommunitycenter.org.

9. For more information, see the websites for the Greensboro Truth and Reconciliation Commission (greensborotrc.org) and Encore.org (encore.org/purpose-prize/nelson-johnson) as well as the film, *Greensboro* (greensborothemovie.com/film/AboutFilm.html).

10. Margaret Moffett, "Greensboro City Council Apologizes for Klan-Nazi Shootings," *News and Record*, August 15, 2017, greensboro.com/news/government/greensboro-city-council-apologizes-for-klan-nazi-shootings/article_f8453871-6ec3-5205-837f-ac4142108483.html.

11. "Tewa Women Unite to Find Healing and Transform Their Communities," W.K. Kellogg Foundation, accessed August 10, 2017, wkkf.org/what-we-do/featured-work/tewa-women-unite-to-find-healing-and-transform-their-communities.

12. Ibid.

13. Tewa Women United, home page, accessed June 4, 2018, tewawomenunited.org.

14. "Real Hero (Fem)," Story People, accessed May 30, 2018, storypeople.com/2018/03/12/real-hero-fem.

15. "Gwendolyn Zoharah Simmons," Veterans of Hope, accessed December 27, 2017, veteransofhope.org/veterans/gwendolyn-zoharah-simmons.

16. Martin Luther King Jr., "Where Do We Go From Here?" *A Testament of Hope: The Essential Writings of Martin Luther King, Jr.*, ed. James Melvin Washington (San Francisco: Harper & Row, Publishers, 1986), 247.

17. "Cornel West Talks to David Shuster," *Aljazeera America*, February 24, 2014, america.aljazeera.com/watch/shows/talk-to-al-jazeera/interviews-and-more/2014/2/24/cornel-west-talkstodavidshuster.html.

18. Emilie Townes, *Breaking the Fine Rain of Death: African American Health Issues and a Womanist Ethic of Care* (New York: Continuum, 2001), 185.

{ Additional Resources }

Video Resources

Life and Debt
lifeanddebt.org

Romero
imdb.com/title/tt0098219

What I Want My Words to Do to You
pbs.org/pov/whatiwant/prison-to-punish-or-reform

Rikers: An American Jail
rikersfilm.org

13th
imdb.com/title/tt5895028

I Am Not Your Negro
imdb.com/title/tt5804038

Restorative Justice in Schools
rethinkingschools.org/articles/restorative-justice

For more information, search for "Restorative Justice in Schools" in a search engine to find videos and articles about how this effort is changing lives.

Greensboro: Closer to the Truth
greensborothemovie.com/film/AboutFilm.html

Children's Defense Fund's Freedom Schools
youtu.be/L3uMwM2hJfw
youtu.be/tzfywLOwxXQ
vimeo.com/71288015

Bibliography and Recommended Reading

Bolded texts are recommended for study leaders.

Alexander, Michelle. *The New Jim Crow: Mass Incarceration in the Age of Colorblindness.* New York: The New Press, 2010.

Barber II, William J. *The Third Reconstruction: Moral Mondays, Fusion Politics, and the Rise of a New Justice Movement.* Boston: Beacon Press, 2016.

Blount, Brian. *Go Preach! Mark's Kingdom Message and the Black Church Today.* Maryknoll, NY: Orbis Books, 1998.

Boff, Leonardo. *The New Evangelization: Good News to the Poor.* Maryknoll, NY: Orbis Books, 1990.

Camp, Lee. *Mere Discipleship: Radical Christianity in a Rebellious World.* Grand Rapids, MI: Brazos Press, 2003.

Campbell, Will. Richard Goode, editor. *Writings on Reconciliation and Resistance.* Eugene, OR: Cascade Books, 2010.

Cardenal, Ernesto. *The Gospel in Solentiname* (4 volumes). Maryknoll, NY: Orbis Books, 1987.

Cone, James. *The Cross and the Lynching Tree.* Maryknoll, NY: Orbis Books, 2011.

Couture, Pamela. *Seeing Children, Seeing God: A Practical Theology of Children and Poverty.* Nashville: Abingdon Press, 2000.

Daley-Harris, Shannon. *Hope for the Future: Answering God's Call to Justice for Our Children.* Louisville: Westminster John Knox Press, 2016.

De Wit, Hans, Louis Jonker, Marleen Kool, Daniel Schipani, editors. *Through the Eyes of Another: Intercultural Reading of the Bible.* Elkhart, IN: Institute of Mennonite Studies, 2004.

Douglas, Kelly Brown. *Stand Your Ground: Black Bodies and the Justice of God.* Maryknoll, NY: Orbis Books, 2015.

Elizondo, Virgilio. *A God of Incredible Surprises.* Lanham, MD: Rowan and Littlefield Publishers, 2003.

Ellison II, Gregory. *Cut Dead but Still Alive: Caring for African American Young Men.* Nashville: Abingdon Press, 2013.

Esquivel, Julia. *Threatened with Resurrection: Prayers and Poems from an Exiled Guatemalan.* Elgin, IL: Brethren Press, 1982, 1994.

Hendricks, Obery. *The Politics of Jesus: Rediscovering the True Revolutionary Nature of the Teachings of Jesus and How They Have Been Corrupted.* New York: Doubleday, 2006.

Isasi-Diaz, Ada Maria. *En la Lucha, In the Struggle: A Hispanic Women's Liberation Theology.* Minneapolis: Fortress Press, 1993.

Jarvis, Cynthia and Elizabeth Johnson, general editors. *Feasting on the Gospels: Mark.* Louisville: Westminster John Knox Press, 2014.

Jennings Jr., Theodore W. *Good News to the Poor: John Wesley's Evangelical Economics.* Nashville: Abingdon Press, 1990.

Jennings Jr., Theodore W. *The Insurrection of the Crucified: The "Gospel of Mark" as Theological Manifesto.* Chicago: Exploration Press, 2003.

Janssen, Denise, editor. *Educating for Redemptive Community.* Eugene, OR: Wipf & Stock, 2015.

Kinsler, Ross and Gloria. *God's Economy: Biblical Studies from Latin America.* Maryknoll, NY: Orbis Books, 2005.

Kinukawa, Hisako. *Women and Jesus in Mark: A Japanese Feminist Perspective.* Maryknoll, NY: Orbis Books, 1994.

Levine, Amy-Jill. *A Feminist Companion to Mark.* Sheffield, England: Sheffield Academic Press, 2001.

Lindner, Eileen. *Thus Far on the Way: Toward a Theology of Child Advocacy.* Louisville: Witherspoon Press, 2006.

Myers, Bryant. *Walking with the Poor: Principles and Practices of Transformational Development.* Maryknoll, NY: Orbis Books, 1999.

Myers, Ched. *The Biblical Vision of Sabbath Economics,* 4th printing. Oak View, CA: Bartimaeus Cooperative Ministries, 2006.

Myers, Ched. *Binding the Strong Man: A Political Reading of Mark's Story of Jesus.* Maryknoll, NY: Orbis Books, 1988.

Myers, Ched, Marie Dennis, Joseph Nanble, Cynthia Moe-Loebeda, and Stuart Taylor. *"Say to This Mountain" Mark's Story of Discipleship.* Maryknoll, NY: Orbis Books, 1996.

Myers, Ched, and Elaine Enns. *Ambassadors of Reconciliation, Volume I: New Testament Reflections on Restorative Justice and Peacemaking. Volume II: Diverse Christian Practices of Restorative Justice and Peacemaking.* Maryknoll, NY: Orbis Books, 2009.

Newsom, Carol, and Sharon Ringe, editors. *Women's Bible Commentary: Expanded Edition with Apocrypha.* Louisville: Westminster John Knox Press, 1998.

Pallares, José Cárdenas. *A Poor Man Called Jesus: Reflections on the Gospel of Mark*. Translated from the Spanish by Robert Barr. Maryknoll, NY: Orbis Books, 1982.

Parker, Evelyn. *The Sacred Selves of Adolescent Girls: Hard Stories of Race, Class, and Gender.* Eugene, OR: Wipf and Stock Press, reprint 2010.

Patte, Daniel, general editor. Severino Coatto, Nicole Wilkinson Duran, Teresa Okure, and Archie Chi Chung Lee, associate editors. *Global Bible Commentary.* Nashville: Abingdon Press, 2004.

Reyes, Patrick. *Nobody Cries When We Die: God, Community and Surviving to Adulthood*. Atlanta: Chalice Press, 2016.

Rhoads, David, Joanna Dewey, and Donali Michie. *Mark as Story: An Introduction to the Narrative of a Gospel*, 3rd edition. Minneapolis: Fortress Press, 2012.

Romero, Oscar. *The Violence of Love*. Maryknoll, NY: Orbis Books, 2007.

St. Clair, Raquel Annette. *Call and Consequences: A Womanist Reading of Mark.* Minneapolis: Fortress Press, 2008.

Salvatierra, Alexia, and Peter Heltzel. *Faith-Rooted Organizing: Mobilizing the Church in Service to the World.* London: Inter-Varsity Press, 2014.

Shopshire, James, Mark Hicks, and Richmond Stoglin, editors. *I Was in Prison: United Methodist Perspective on Prison Ministry.* Nashville: General Board of Higher Education and Ministry, The United Methodist Church, 2008.

Soelle, Dorothee. *The Silent Cry: Mysticism and Resistance*. Minneapolis: Fortress, 2001.

Song, C.S. *Jesus and the Reign of God.* Minneapolis: Augsberg Press, 1993.

Smith, Mitzi. *I Found God in Me: A Womanist Biblical Hermeneutics Reader.* Eugene, OR: Cascade Books, 2015.

Stevenson, Bryan. *Just Mercy: A Story of Justice and Redemption.* New York: Spiegel & Grau, 2014.

Tamez, Elsa. *Bible of the Oppressed.* New York: Orbis Books, 1982.

Thurman, Howard. *Jesus and the Disinherited.* Boston: Beacon Press, 1949; reprint, 1949.

Tolbert, Mary Ann. *Sowing the Gospel: Mark's World in Literary-Historical Perspective.* Minneapolis: Augsberg Press, 1989.

Washington, James Melvin, editor. *A Testament of Hope: The Essential Writings of Martin Luther King, Jr.* San Francisco: Harper & Row, Publishers, 1986.

West, Traci. *Disruptive Christian Ethics: When Racism and Women's Lives Matter.* Louisville: Westminster John Knox Press, 2006.

Williams, Chad, Kidada Williams, and Keisha Blain, editors. *Charleston Syllabus: Readings on Race, Racism, and Racial Violence.* Athens: University of Georgia Press, 2016.

Wink, Walter. *Engaging the Powers: Discernment and Resistance in a World of Domination.* Minneapolis: Augsberg Press, 1992.

Wong, Kent, Ana Luz Gonzalez, and James M. Lawson Jr. *Nonviolence and Social Movements: The Teachings of Rev. James M. Lawson Jr.* Los Angeles: UCLA Center for Labor Research and Education, 2016.

{ About the Author }

Janet Wolf has lived in Nashville, Tennessee, since 1968. After working for twelve years as a community organizer around poverty rights, she received her MDiv from Vanderbilt Divinity School and was ordained as an elder in The United Methodist Church in 1988. She served as a pastor of rural and urban congregations for twelve years. In 2001, Janet was appointed as director of public policy and community outreach with Religious Leaders for a More Just and Compassionate Drug Policy, a national interfaith coalition working on harm reduction, alternatives to incarceration, and restorative justice.

In 2005, Janet was appointed to American Baptist College, a historically black college in Nashville, where she served as a full-time professor and interim academic dean. In July 2012, she was appointed to work with Marian Wright Edelman and the Children's Defense Fund, focusing on nonviolent, direct-action organizing to dismantle the cradle-to-prison pipeline, including Children's Defense Fund's Freedom Schools and the annual Samuel DeWitt Proctor Institute.

Janet is a partner with several think tanks inside prisons and a co-facilitator with insiders in courses on death row and in maximum security. She is also part of a teaching team working to provide undergraduate and seminary courses taught inside prisons. She was co-creator of a DMin program in prisons, public policy, and transformative justice at New Brunswick Theological Seminary, New Jersey, in which she was both a professor and a student, graduating with a DMin in 2015.

She is the author of "To See and To Be Seen," a chapter in *I Was in Prison: United Methodist Perspectives on Prison Ministry* edited by James M. Shopshire Sr., Richmond Stoglin, and Mark C. Hicks (Nashville: General Board of Higher Education and Ministry, 2008).

Janet is married to Bill Haley, a retired public school teacher and former legal services director, and they have five sons and six grandchildren.

NOTES